The MANSFIELD RIOTS of 1900

The MANSFIELD RIOTS of 1900

Second Edition

by

Robert A. Carter

EMBLEM OF THE "MANSFIELD BLUES."

All Rights Reserved. No part of this publication may be reproduced or transmitted in any form or by any means, electronic or technical, including photocopying, recording, or by any information storage or retrieval system, without permission in writing from the publisher, except by a reviewer who may quote brief passages in a review.

Copyright © Robert A. Carter 2009, 2024

Rights to photographs and illustrations retained by owners as indicated.

Photo Credits:
Bob Vail Collection, 5
Century Magazine (Dec. 1906), 93
Chicago Historical Society, 50, 60, 109, 115
Crestline Public Library, 92
Library of Congress, 113
Mansfield Fire Museum, 17
Mansfield Memorial Museum, 6, 33
Mansfield Police Department Archives, 16, 69
Mark Hertzler Collection, 7-8, 12, 39-40
Phil Stoodt Collection, 18, 27, 34, 37, 80, 94
Richland County Chapter, Ohio Genealogical Society, 18, 27, 34, 37, 80, 94
Richland County Historical Soceity, 20, 28, 43
Robert Carter Collection, 11, 15, 21, 29, 42, 46, 76, 96, 99
Sherman Room, Microfilm/ M/Richland County Public Library, 9-10, 13-14, 24-25, 31-32, 35-36, 38, 41, 44-45, 48, 51, 53, 56-57, 61-64, 66-68, 70-73, 76-79, 81-82, 95, 97-98, 102-103
Zion Historical Society, 3, 21, 26, 30, 47, 52, 54, 59, 85, 89, 106, 108, 111-112, 114
Zion Scrapbooks, Newberry Library, Chicago, 4, 49, 55, 58, 74, 83-84, 86-87, 90-91, 105, 107

The Mansfield Riots of 1900

by

Robert A. Carter

Second Edition

ISBN 978-1-7361884-5-3

www.turaspublishing.com

. . . we shall not escape a brawl;
For now, these hot days, is the mad blood
stirring.

William Shakespeare
Romeo and Juliet
Act III. Scene I.

Table of Contents

List of Figures viii

Preface xi

Chapter 1   The Gathering Storm 1

Chapter 2   Elder Fockler Returns 11

Chapter 3   Another Outbreak of Mob Violence. 24

Chapter 4   Meanwhile, Back at the Ranch 43

Chapter 5   Just Tell Them You Saw Me 55

Chapter 6   Divine Healing and Habes Corpus. Divine Healing? . 65

Chapter 7   About Petered Out 71

Chapter 8   Downie Lands in England 78

Chapter 9   Mansfield Troubles Continues 83

Chapter 10 The Turning Point 93

Post Script - The Rise and Fall of Dowie 102

The Last Word - Glorious Victory 112

Index 115

The Author 117

List of Figures

1. Mansfield Blues Emblem i
2. Post Office Stamp iii
3. Elder Cyrus B. Fockler 2
4. John Alexander Dowie 3
5. Christian Catholic Church 4
6. Women Employed in Mansfield 5
7. A.J. Rigby Cigar Maker 5
8. H. L. Bowers Company 5
9. Elder Fockler Headlines 7
10. Hunginton Brown 8
11. Sheriff A. B. "Barney" Pulver 9
12. Richland County Jail 9
13. Dowie Letter to Mayor Brown 10
14. Pawnee Bill's Wild West 11
15. The Vonhof Hotel 12
16. The Mansfield Police Department 13
17. Fireman "Doss" Dell and the Department's Hose Wagon 14
18. Mansfield's Prison 16
19. The Methodist Church on the Square 17
20. The E.L. Miller Livery and Cab Service 18
21. William Hammer Piper 20
22. Telegram from John Alexander Dowie. 21
23. Telegram from Ohio Governor George K. Nash 21
24. *Leaves of Healing* 22
25. Dowie's Church Newspaper 23
26. The Four Zion Preachers 24
27. The Roderick Lear Harlow Works 25
28. The Blue Elders 26
29. Mary Pulver 28
30. Damage to the Frederick Home 29
31. Front Page of Mansfield's Newspapers 30
32. Mansfield Attorney A. A. Douglass 32
33. Union Depot—Mansfield, Ohio 33
34. President McKinley and Governor Nash 34
35. B&O Depot 34
36. Crowd at B&O Railroad 35
37. The Tremont House Hotel 36
38. Mayor Brown Cartoon 36
39. Young Women Working in Mansfield Industries 37
40. Young Women Working in Cigar Factories, etc. 37
41. Mansfield Fire Department at the City Building 38
42. Telegram 39
43. Elbow-Benders and Bartenders in Local Saloons 40
44. Crowds at Train Station 41
45. Ashland gets Unwelcome Visitors 41

List of Figures - *Continued*

46. Richland County Sheriff A. A. Barney Pulver 42
47. Dowie's First Tabernacle in America. 43
48. Dowie's Use of the Word Catholic 44
49. Zion Headquarters in Chicago 44
50. Use of the Chicago Auditorium 45
51. Religious Tract 47
52. Dowie Discovery of a Vile Plot 47
53. Central Zion Tabernacle, Chicago 48
54. Dowie on Stage 49
55. Typical Dowie Altar 50
56. Dowie's *Leaves of Healing* 51
57. Mansfield's Masonic Temple 51
58. Hamilton Brown 51
59. Dowie Family Portrait 52
60. Dowie Speaks from his Private Railroad Car 53
61. Dowie Caricature 54
62. Richland County Law Library 55
63. Company M of the Ohio National Guard 56
64. *Leaves of Healing* 57
65. The Former Home of E. H. Leiby 58
66. The Splash of Daid Staunch 59
67. Mansfield Blues 60
68. Newspapers Sense of Humor 61
69. Chief Barrett Replaces Chief Clark 62
70. Vicious Cartoon in *Leaves of Healing* 62
71. *Mansfield News* Cartoons 63
72. *Mansfield News* Cartoon "Happy Home" 63
73. *Mansfield News* Cartoon of Chief Barrett 64
74. Mansfield in *Cleveland World* 67
75. The Old Methodist Church 68
76. Dowie Elders and Deacons Arrive by Train 69
77. Some Incidents of Dowie Troubles 70
78. Overseer Piper 72
79. The Buggy Works Near Union Station 73
80. The Mansfield Square 74
81. Streets Teeming with People 74
82. Bassinger and Muth Cartoon 75
83. Newspaper Reports Across the Country 76
84. Newspaper Reports Across the Country 76
85. John Alexander Dowie 79
86. "Chicago Mystery Man" 80
87. Dowie Shielded by Police 81
88. Dowie as the Prophet of Profit 82
89. No Dowieites Need Apply 83
90. William Hamner Piper—Dowie's Number Two Man 84

List of Figures - *Continued*

91. Mansfield Blues Button 84
92. The Continental Hotel in Crestline 85
93. Dr. John Speicher 87
94. The Brunswick Hotel 88
95. The Plight of Elder Williams 90
96. The Richland County Jail 92
97. *Leave of Healing* Blasts Mayor Brown 93
98. Funeral of John Sherman 95
99. Company M Marches Quietly 96
100. Services for John Sherman 97
101. Photo from John Angle's Grocery Store 98
102. An Incident at the Train 98
103. A Crowd at Union Station Bids Dowies "Don't Come Back" 99
104. Final Word to All Citizens 101
105. Dowie Sketch of his Proposed Temple .103
106. Grand Plan for Zion City 103
107. Location of Zion City 104
108. Shiloh House —Dowie's Mansion 104
109. 350-Room Hotel Built in About Three Months 105
110. Zion Lace Sample 106
111. General Overseer's Elaborate "Elijah II" Costume 107
112. Dowie Passing Through on the B&O in his Private Car 108
113. Dowie's Return to Zion City in 1904 109
114, The Lace Factory 110
115. No Smoking in Zion City 111
116. Dowie Men Who "Suffered and Conquered" at Mansfield 112
117. More Dowie Men Who "Suffered and Conquered" at Mansfield 113

Preface

In 1900 the city of Mansfield, with a population of 17,640, was a bustling, growing Midwestern city surrounded by rich farm lands and railroads that connected it's business and industrial interests with the rest of the country. Writer Louis Bromfield once called the place "Little Chicago." The steel mill, Altman & Taylor Company, Eclipse Stove Company, Ohio Brass and the Lean Farm Tool were just a few heavy industries that offered employment for men, while the National Biscuit Company, Tracey & Avery, the Bissman Company and a surprising number of cigar and suspender manufacturers offered jobs for women and children. Retail stores also began to offer employment for young women.

The working class for the most part lived in areas north and east of the square while the more affluent resided south and to the west side. The movers and shakers, the wealthy or well-off, took up residence on Park Avenue West, Marion Avenue or West Fourth Street.

When Huntington Brown was elected mayor in 1899 he had no premonition of what terrible situation would befall his administration the following year. It tested him as well as other elected officials, including Richland County Sheriff A. B. "Barney" Pulver and Ohio Governor George K. Nash It was all caused by an Elder, a preacher from Chicago, and the resulting riots gained wide national attention in the press which gave Mansfield a bit of a black eye.

In this day and age it is hard to imagine the unrest and unbelievable mob action against a new church whose members were denounced and leaders were coated with tar and feathers. The Christian Catholic Church, founded by John Alexander Dowie of Chicago, managed to bring that situation upon themselves in the summer of 1900. At times it was more than the Mayor, the Sheriff and the police could handle.

Newspaper accounts of those troubled times are very often quoted in this book. They were the chief source of information. The writer feels they lend the flavor of reporter's eyewitness account and editor's somewhat slanted views. There was also competition between the two principal local newspapers to outdo each other.

A scrapbook collection of news clippings found at the Newberry Library in Chicago contains a wealth of information on Dowie's exploits in both the United States and Great Britain. The Sherman Room of the Mansfield/Richland County Public Library holds the remnants of Mayor Huntington Brown's scrapbook and local newspaper microfilm files. Staff members Boyd Addlesperger and Laurel Tope were most helpful in locating information for this book.

Timothy Brian McKee, who has written books of his own, assembled a series of photographs from many sources that not only identify people and locations involved in this story, but also take the reader back in time to a Mansfield that is barely recognizable today. The illustrations make this publication much more immediate and interesting. It was his graphic skills in putting together these pages for the printer that bring the story to life.

D. W. Garber, the writer and historian, really set this project in motion back in 1968 when he gave the author an inch-thick hand-typed folder copied from the *Mansfield Shield & Banner* covering the summer of 1900. This was done in the day before photocopies or microfilm came along, and he typed every word and highlighted important items pertaining to the Dowie troubles. Garber wrote a book for the Ohio Historical Society, *Waterwheels and Mill Stones, a History of Mills and Milling in Ohio*, 1970. He generously gave the Dowie material to me. In a way, he was my teacher. His file was my textbook.

The other source of inspiration for this work was the writer's grandmother, Mary Pulver Carter, who was the oldest daughter of Sheriff A. B. "Barney" Pulver. As an 18 year old teenager in 1900 she saved many news items and important telegrams her father received and pasted them into her scrapbook. The book is now the family treasure.

Robert Carter, 2009

Chapter 1

The Gathering Storm

In August of 1899, the mistreatment of a two-year old boy would lead to one of the most explosive episodes in the history of Mansfield. A front page headline and detailed story in the August 10, 1899, edition of the *Mansfield Daily Shield* grabbed the attention of readers:

> Cyrus Fockler, the traveling apostle of what he calls the Catholic Church of Christ, who has been working the faith cure racket on a little two-year old boy of Frank D. Calver of 219 East Second Street, was locked up Wednesday afternoon on the complaint of Dr. Boles. He attempted to interfere with Dr. Boles in his care of the child which has been ill with cholera and inflammation of the bowels for the past week and for whose recovery there is now little hope on account of the outrageous care given the little fellow.
>
> Dr. Boles was called to look into the case by Health Officer Craig Tuesday at 11 p.m. He found the child dangerously ill and so notified the family who refused to accept the doctor's statement and refused to administer the medicine prescribed. Wednesday morning Dr. Boles left medicine a second time and he entertained grave fears that the medicines were not being given according to directions. Of this fact he notified Dr. Craig that the faith curist Fockler was interfering and preventing the family from administering medicine left for the relief of the child.

Surprisingly, after Fockler was arrested the family still refused to follow the doctor's orders, so a nurse was sent to stay the night with instructions to let no one but the parents into the boy's room. One parent commented, "Now they are going to give him poison and he will surely die."

> The Calvers' were members of a church organized and ruled by John Alexander Dowie of Chicago. The services of a doctor or druggist were forbidden and, according to Dowie, all that was needed to heal the sick was prayer and faith in God. There were growing numbers of converts in Mansfield.

Newspapers in that era often crafted personal opinions into their stories. One reporter blatantly included this judgement:

> This is one of the most outrageous things that has ever occurred in the city of Mansfield and that sane people can be so far tricked and fooled by such a dastardly attempt at murder under the cloak of pretended Christianity is a thing hard to believe and certainly will not be condoned by the city officials.

Fockler appeared in mayor's court with his Mansfield attorney, A. A. Douglass. Douglass entered a plea of not guilty for his client and asked that he be bound over to a higher court. The courtroom was packed, mostly with Fockler's supporters, and a bond of $2,500 was set for each of three counts as follows:

First, causing physical pain and mental suffering of a child.

Second, for torturing and cruelly punishing a child and endangering his life and health.

Third, for interfering with an officer.

Fockler remained in jail for the night until his $7,500 bond could be raised. This was a stiff amount but the defendant lived in Canton and Mayor Huntington Brown, like many others, were disgusted with the whole case. Brown wanted him in court to face a jury. Fockler had been involved in another similar case with a small child earlier but had not been arrested. Brown also suggested that the ministers throughout the city take up the faith healing subject for their sermon next Sunday. This was a serious subject bound to generate much discussion.

Another inkling of the coming storm was also noted in the *Mansfield News* in November of 1899 when Al Moore, the Lexington Correspondent, repeated remarks of George Frye, a Chicago businessman and son of a Lexington Presbyterian Minister, who wrote of John Alexander Dowie's exploits in an October 1899 issue of an unidentified Chicago newspaper.

It was a critical analysis of the character of the self-appointed vicar of God. He exposed in a clear manner Dowie's methods to enrich himself from the possessions of unsophisticated religious enthusiasts. It was Mr. Frye who started the crusade to disenthrone Dowie.

Elder Cyrus B. Fockler

Fig. 3. Elder Fockler created a storm of protest the likes of which had never been experienced in Mansfield. (Zion Historical Society)

Over a four-year period Fry had occasionally attended Dowie's Chicago church and, although not a member, with his religious and business background he could see what Dowie was up to.

John Alexander Dowie was born in Edinburgh, Scotland in 1847. His parents moved to Adeladie, Australia, in 1860, and as a young man worked in a dry goods business. At age

20 he returned to the University of Edinburgh and studied the ministry. In 1870 he was ordained as a minister in the Congregational Church in Alma, Australia, and in a few years was able to build a large tabernacle in Melbourne. During his several pastorates he began to fancy his supposed ability to heal through prayer, and this became the basis of his evangelistic work. This came about when he was called to comfort the parents of a young girl near death. A doctor in attendance had called her case hopeless. As he prayed for some time over the feverous dying girl she awoke and was healed. Word of this spread and others came to Dowie for help.

In 1888 he moved to San Francisco, where after two years gained little success, and then moved to Chicago. Here he gained support by preaching against and condemning doctors, druggists, secret societies, liquor, pork, tobacco and, in particular, any and all other religious denominations. In 1895 a group of Chicago clergymen and physicians filed more than

Fig. 4. Newspapers in the United States and Great Britain carried stories of Dowie's rise to prominence and wealth. Even their negative coverage served to promote him. (Zion Scrapbooks, Newberry Library, Chicago.)

one hundred charges against him but Dowie won every case. There was no law against faith healing. The ill-advised court proceedings served only to advertise him. In 1896 the Christian Catholic Church in Zion was formed with Dowie as General Overseer. Prone to exaggeration, by 1900 he would claim 50,000 followers, who were required to give ten percent of their income to the church or face immediate expulsion. Dowie controlled all church assets and ruled with an iron hand. The services of a doctor or druggist were forbidden. Membership in the Masons or any other "secret" society was banned, as was attending dance halls or theaters. Strict obedience was demanded and failure to obey resulted in expulsion.

A congregation of Dowie's new sect formed in Mansfield originally in the late 1890s that met in member homes and, as the congregation grew, leased a hall at the corner of Park Avenue East and Adams Street. It was called Zion Tabernacle, and the first meetings were held in early May of 1900; but a couple of weeks later, while the sanctuary was being remodeled, the congregation used the Universalist Church on East Third Street for evening services only. Initially harmony existed between churches but that soon ended. In June the growing Zion congregation rented the Casino at North Lake Park for Sunday services.

STINK POTS?

Animosity towards the Dowie church quickly took root, spurred on by the behavior of Elder Cyrus Fockler, the head of the Mansfield branch. Fockler strongly criticized and condemned almost every other denomination in town. In addition Fockler called all the young women employed in the shops and factories "fallen women or stink pots" implying they were prostitutes or of poor moral character, used liquor or smoked tobacco. Those who indulged in the latter two were labeled "stink pots."

Mansfield was a leading manufacturer of suspenders in the United States. In addition there were numerous cigar makers in town, all of which employed large numbers of young women. Nearly 1,000 working girls were thus employed in various industries throughout Mansfield and one community leader noted that behind every one of these women there were usually four male defenders; her father, two brothers and a special fellow. That meant that there were 4,000 men ready to protect the womens' good names.

Fig. 5. The Casino building in North Lake Park was used for conventions, shows, dances and other events. The large hall was rented temporarily by the Christian Catholic Church in Zion for Sunday services. (Bob Vail collection.)

Fig. 6. Nearly 1000 young women were employed in Mansfield shops and factories. The largest number was either making cigars or men's suspenders while numerous others toiled in the stores, offices or markets. (Mansfield Memorial Museum)

Figs. 7 and 8. Between 1900 and 1906 there were at least 15 cigar manufacturing concerns in Mansfield, and one cigar box maker. A.J. Rigby on East Third Street was the largest cigar maker and no doubt many women employees went home with brown fingers. The most popular cigars in town were those called Bill William manufactured by the H. L. Bowers Company. (Mark Hertzler collection)

The controversy started to boil, in a July 6, 1900 issue of the *The Mansfield Daily Shield* which carried the headline:

> **Fockler Figures In Another Case**
>
> Another case in which Cyrus B. Fockler of Zion fame figures prominently has come to the notice of the authorities during the past couple of days and a full investigation was made by Coroner Bushnell.
>
> On July 4 the six-weeks-old child of Mr. and Mrs. Charles Bauer of 194 East Third St. died after "being treated with prayer" by Fockler. The matter was reported to the Health Officer Craig, who referred the case to Coroner Bushnell.
>
> Thursday Coroner Bushnell went to the Bauer home where he found the child had died of convulsions. There had been no physician called in the case as Fockler was endeavoring to demonstrate his ability as a divine healer. Coroner Bushnell was of the opinion that the life of the child might have been saved had it received proper medical treatment. He took the parents of the child to task and told them that the time would come when so called faith healers and parents would answer to the charge of manslaughter for such criminal negligence.
>
> Coroner Bushnell then consulted with Prosecutor Bowers in regard to the case and found the statutes did not cover such a case and there will be no arrests made at present. Bushnell was highly indignant over the affair and stated to the Shield man that he will endeavor to secure introduction of a bill into the state legislature which will break up this practice of "divine healing" in this state.
>
> Mrs. Bauer is a devoted member of Zion tabernacle but Mr. Bauer, because he refused to contribute tithes to Dowie, it is claimed, (consisting of one-tenth of his income) was dropped from membership.
>
> The man Fockler has figured prominently in several cases similar to this which he refused to allow a physician to be called, claiming all that was needed was his treatment by prayer. Until something can be done under the law it is very probable that the population of the cemetery will continue to increase more rapidly than necessary.

The death of the Bauer infant and the news story lit the fuse. Cyrus Fockler kept it going the following Sunday, July 8, when he delivered a bitter tirade at the Casino against Mansfield officials and the newspaper which carried this story:

> Cyrus B. Fockler, of "Dowie's Zion", delivered a violent tirade of abuse against the doctors, druggist, Health Officer Craig, Coroner Bushnell and the Shield at the Casino Sunday afternoon, before an audience of about 50 people.
>
> The prelude to Fockler's address was advertised to be "The Lies of the Devil's Shield Exposed." The occasion for this was an article which appeared in Friday's Shield in regard to the death of the little Bauer child of East Third St. A Shield man was present at the Casino and was completely disgusted with the filthy language used by

this man, which is unprintable, to say the least. Fockler brought a copy of the Shield article on stage and commented on it in language more violent than elegant. Fockler had his audience trained to respond to his questions, and resembled in detail a puppet show. For example, Fockler would ask; "What are the druggists?" The people would answer, "Sorcerers." Fockler would grin benignly.

Fockler delivered a bitter tirade against Elder Johnson of the Methodist Church and branded him an "ignoramus." The reporter noted that the man on the stage often used the words "hain't" and "aint" which seemed rather ill-fitting for one who called the learned Methodist minister an "ignoramus."

Fig. 9. Elder Fockler made headlines again on July 6, 1900 and a reporter crafted his opinion into his story indicating an increase in the cemetery business. (Sherman Room microfilm, M/RCPL)

That same day Charles Bauer went to Mayor Huntington Brown's office and angrily complained about the treatment he and his wife had received from Fockler. His wife was bedridden with nerves over the loss of her child and on the day of the funeral, a doctor was summoned. Fockler objected and attempted to force his way into the house. He told her if she took medicine she would die. When Bauer returned home from an errand, he found Fockler and three followers holding funeral services over the dead infant without his knowledge or consent.

Mayor Brown said there was nothing he could do under the law but suggested Bauer get a club and "give Fockler a good beating the next time he crosses your threshold." Mayor Brown was a practical man.

The *Daily Shield* continued with this upsetting item:

> While the Mayor and Prosecutor Bowers were talking to Bauer the telephone rang and Eb Ford informed the Mayor that Mrs. Frank Dell of Benton Street, a devout follower of Zion tabernacle, was on her way down the street acting queerly. Mayor Brown then directed Chief Clark and Officer McKay to be on the lookout for her. They found her ten minutes later in the park talking religion and seemingly raving mad. A large crowd soon gathered and the unfortunate woman was taken to the women's department of the county jail for safe keeping.
>
> The crowd of excited citizens who gathered were highly indignant and threats were made against the inhuman monster who has been the direct cause of death of innocent babes, wrecked homes and insane loved ones. It is said that when Fockler finds

> a husband will not embrace his "religion" he endeavors to cause estrangement between husband and wife and in more than one case has been successful.
>
> Chief Clark swore out a lunacy affidavit against Mrs. Dell this morning. It will be remembered that Fockler attended Mrs. Dell in childbirth sometime ago and the child died.

And then the news coverage ended with this incendiary statement:

> It is not known how long this state of affairs will continue as the authorities are helpless but suffice to say that something should be done quickly to prevent this fellow from working further harm in Mansfield.

THINGS GET UGLY

That, as it turned out, was the starting gun for mob action. The following day a mob of "infuriated" citizens met at the town square and hatched a plan to capture Fockler, tar and feather him and ride him out of town on a rail. They had everything they needed!

Fig. 10. Mansfield's newly elected bachelor Mayor Huntington Brown may have entertained thoughts that a mob of irate citizens would quickly put an end to the Zion elders outrageous remarks. He was wrong. (Sherman Room collection, M/RCPL)

They decided to pay Fockler a surprise visit at his home at 9:00 that evening. At the stroke of 9 PM a mob estimated between 250 and 500 men and boys in a rather quiet compact group moved down the north side of Park Avenue East, paused at the Zion Church to make sure Fockler was not there, and then on south to Second Street arriving at the home of Enoch H. Leiby, 209 East Second where Folkner was staying. Fortunately for Fockler, he had gone back to Chicago earlier to see Dowie but the mob leaders loudly insisted in searching the Leiby house anyway. Leiby finally allowed one person to enter and look. Many were not satisfied and remained in the area for some time. Then with their tar buckets, feathers and a long wooden rail they finally went home.

Sheriff "Barney" Pulver was called for help during the mob's action but refused to interfere saying it was out of his jurisdiction, even though he could possibly see the Leiby home from an upper jail house window. The police were called but all officers were "in the southern part of the city." One gets the impression that law enforcement thought if they looked the other way all problems with Elder Fockler would be taken care of and go away. If they did, they were wrong.

On July 20, Dowie sent a long letter to Mayor Huntington Brown commenting on the lengthy articles in the press, especially the *Shield,* which made him aware of the abusive and unwarranted language concerning Elder Fockler. He pointed out that the members of the Christian Catholic Church in Zion had broken no laws, and he vowed to hold

Fig. 11. Newly elected Sheriff A. B. "Barney" Pulver had previously served as a Richland County Tax Assassor and had little training for the situation that was developing. He was a friend of Senator John Sherman and a leader among the local Republicans. (Robert Carter collection)

authorities responsible for damage to property and injuries to his Elder in Mansfield. The letter ended with this:

> **Trusting that you and the authorities under you will do your duty and maintain the rights of all and prevent all mob violence, which is a disgrace to a civilized community, I am**
>
> **John Alexander Dowie**

The letter was printed in the *Daily Shield*.

The Zion church newspaper Leaves of Healing was distributed all over town a few days later and, although a "church" publication, it in sometimes colorful foul language denounced the mob, the mayor, the police, the clergy and nearly everyone else.

That must have caused some tight jaws and lowered eyebrows. At the same time Coroner Bushnell made his finding public in the case of the dead Bauer baby.

> **I find that the baby came to his death through convulsions. I further find that the child had been treated unlawfully by Cyrus B. Fockler and I believe that if the child had received proper medical treatment it might have lived.**

George Laver, the owner of the building on Park Avenue East that was then being remodeled for use as the Zion Tabernacle, ordered all work to be stopped by the carpenters, electricians and paper hangers. He stated the

Fig. 12. The Richland County Jail stood next to the court house and was torn down when the present court house was built. As was the custom, the Sheriff and his family stayed in the living quarters. Mrs. Pulver and her oldest daughter cooked for and fed the prisoners. (Mark Hertzler collection)

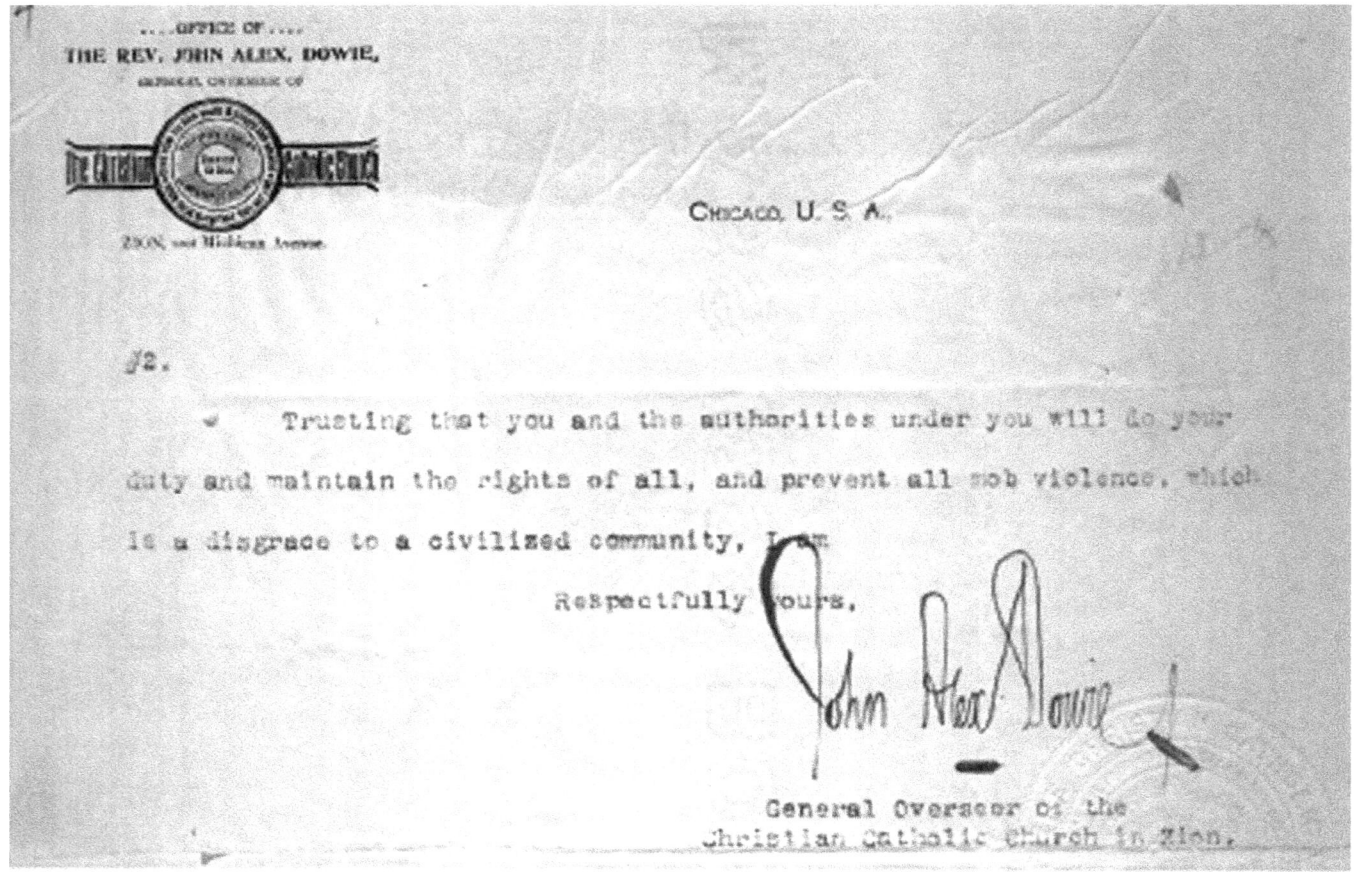

Fig. 13. John Aleander Dowie sent a respectful personal letter to Mayor Brown asking for protection of his Elder's rights. It seems evident from his signature that he had no modest opinion of himself. (Huntington Brown scrapbook, Sherman Room collection, M/RCPL)

building would no longer be used by Fockler and his Zion congregation. Money spent on the work was to be returned to Fockler. It is easy to speculate that Laver came under strong criticism for having leased the place to Fockler in the first place. Given the growing hostility toward Fockler, Laver had a growing concern that his building might be vandalized.

Mrs. Dell was released from jail at the request of relatives and taken to the country to be cared for by them. When Sheriff Pulver and Deputy Sheriff Tom Bell went after her for the hearing she was found wandering up and down the lane talking religion. Escorted into Judge Brinkerhoff's court for a lunacy hearing by her husband and aged mother she was a pitiful sight. As reported in the *Mansfield Daily Shield*:

> **Mrs. Dell became hysterical and created a scene. There is no question that Mrs. Dell is insane and it is feared that hers is a hopeless case. It was a pathetic scene, the aged white-haired mother compelled to witness the examination of her daughter for lunacy—all brought on by Fockler. Mrs. Dell will be examined by Dr. Baughman and then will be taken to the Toledo Asylum. Mrs. Dell stated in court that she and Fockler would go hand and hand to heaven. (If the citizens once get their hands on**

Fockler he is very likely to go hand over hand upwards—but not to heaven).Indignation against Fockler runs high in all quarters and if he returns to Mansfield he is in danger of being treated to a coat of tar and feathers which he richly deserves. It is stated that Fockler is to return to Mansfield Thursday from Canton.

These inflammatory statements by an idiot reporter and approved by the not overly-bright editor William Lawrence, led to the mob riot the next day.

Chapter 2
Elder Fockler Returns

Fockler came back to Mansfield with another Dowie Elder E. P. Fisher. A crowd had daily been gathering at the railroad station watching for Fockler but it was a night for a scant mob. It seemed that most folks were at the fairgrounds watching Pawnee Bill's Wild West Show. Only a few men were at the station.

After the two men registered at the Vonhof Hotel, Fockler, with his hired Mansfield attorney A. A. Douglass, went to Mayor Brown's office where Douglass demanded police protection for his client. Fockler then walked over to the lawyer's office in the Newman Building. Shortly thereafter a crowd began to gather outside. Although he had shaved his beard and mustache to alter his appearance Fockler was still recognized on the streets. The crowd grew in Central Park and every exit to the building was watched but Fockler made a quick exit out a rear door and ran ahead of his pursuers back to the Vonhof.

What happened next was reported in local newspapers adequately enough, but a detailed firsthand account authored by Elder Fockler himself, printed in a late July issue of *Leaves of Healing*, is quoted here.

> **We went directly to our room, and there silently prayed and consulted to the best course to pursue. We soon saw them filling the alley, climbing up on buildings, and heard them yelling in the street below. We went out in the hall, where the proprietor of the hotel met us and said that we should not have come there, and that we had better go down the fire-escape the back way. We told him that we would do nothing of the kind, and that we were there as his guests and expected protection. He went down and we were left alone in the hall.**

Fig. 14. Had Mansfielders known what real-life "wild west" events they were about to witness in their own town in the following weeks, they might not have spent 25 cents to watch actors who only pretended violence. (Sherman Room microfilm, M/RCPL)

We talked with them probably five minutes. While we were speaking to them at the rear of the hall, where there is a fire-escape, they began to appear at the window, and soon were coming in to the number of about fifteen or more. I asked them what they had against me, and they said that I had called those who used tobacco "stinkpots," and that I said that we could smell the odor of tobacco on the girls who worked in the cigar factories as they passed us on the streets.

They also said that I called druggists "sorcerers." They also said that I hypnotized, or put some kind of power over the people, and had spoken against Secret Societies; and other similarly foolish charges. One of them asked why I did not preach as other preachers did.

The leader then drew out his watch and said to Evangelist Fisher, "We will give you five minutes' time to leave this city." Evangelist Fisher said he would do nothing of the kind, and he stood faithfully by me.

One then cried, "What is the use of talking any more?" Whereupon they seized me, and the entire number hustled me down the flight of stairs. When we came into the main hall we saw the entire street filled with a sea of faces. Some cried one thing and some another.

In a very vicious manner they forced me out into the street. Immediately three or four policemen began to try to protect me against the howling mob. They cried, "Let him speak!" I waited, raised my hands and waited for them to become quiet. But the moment I began to speak, they gave a yell, and in a moment or two there was a mad rush and I was separated from the police. With vicious hands upon me I was forced to run about three-fourths of a mile to the gas house with the mob yelling.

My coat and hat were torn off me in front of the hotel, and when we came to the gas house they immediately forced me into the house and began to cry for tar, but failed to find any. While inside they viciously tore my clothes from my body, ripping them into shreds, with the exception of the clothes from my waist down. In a few minutes they hurried me out of the

Fig. 15. The Vonhof on North Main Street was the largest and finest hotel in Mansfield. Located a short distance from the Square, it offered weary travelers good rooms, a bar and restaurant for $2 a night. Note the fire escape stair on the right that figured in Fokler's abduction. (Robert Carter collection)

Fig. 16. The Mansfield Police Department posed for this photograph early in 1900, evidently before the Dowie trouble began when more officers were deputized. Unfortunately the officers are not identified, but the man in the derby hat was Chief Clark. (Mansfield Police Department archives)

house into the back yard, and there, seeing a vat of tar, and thinking it might be soft, they threw me into it.

But it was of a solid nature and bore me up, and I leaped out of it again.

They again seized me and took me to a pump in the yard and forced me under it and began to pump, supposing that tar would issue from the pump. But, for some unknown reason nothing came from the pump.

The engineer then fought nobly for me, and assisted me in various ways, speaking kindly words to me through the entire following scenes. The police, five or six in number, did their duty nobly as far as I could see. I was then hurried back into the building, where scenes similar to the others transpired, and they demanded of me whether I would leave the city. After a moment's hesitation, knowing that I could truthfully say Yes, I said I would, and the officers told them that I would leave.

But it was to no avail. They still cried, "Kill him!" "Lynch him!" "Hang him!" etc.

Fig. 17. Fireman "Doss" Dell used the department's hose wagon to rescue elder Fockler and haul a couple of cops away from the angry mob. They are pictured here in front of the old Number 2 station on North Main Street. (Mansfield Fire Museum)

The officers and the engineer began hurrying me out into the yard, and I was hurried down to a three-foot stone wall, where there was a vicious fight for the possession of my body. At this place all the clothing was torn in shreds from my body, nothing remaining upon my person but my shoes and stockings. Some one of the mob took hold of my right foot and began with a rush to drag me from the police, but God helped me to keep in an upright position, and in a few minutes more my foot was released. Then the officers saw that they could not force their way through the crowd, but succeeded in getting me up on top of the wall and inside of the yard.

At that moment the fire alarm was sounded and the hose cart with firemen responded. The new recruit of officers came rushing to my assistance. One of them drew his revolver and cried at the top of his voice, "Men, stand back or I will fire on you and shoot you dead." I then, with others, said to him, "Do not shoot—put down your gun." A desperate fight then ensued for the possession of my body, in which the policemen and many citizens, among whom were some of he doctors of the town, and many others that I did not know, did all that they could to protect me and rescue me.

> Some one passed the word to the driver of the fire wagon to drive close to the wall, which he did, and then, with a heroic effort on the part of the officers and citizens, the crowd was forced back and I was aided to get on the wagon and four officers jumped on, and the driver drove with desperate speed toward the city prison, the mob following after with great speed and screaming all the way. We reached the prison only about two minutes before they did, and I was safely behind the bars with nothing on my body but a coat that had been handed to me after I got upon the wagon, from some one in the crowd. The mob then climbed upon adjoining buildings and surged around the prison trying to catch a glimpse of me, but I kept myself in such a position that they could not see me, by direction of the officers.
>
> A number of doctors, among whom was Dr. Craig, came in to see me. He shook hands with me and gave me an expression of his sympathy. He said that he felt that this was an outrage and a shame. I asked him in the presence of the people if he was not called to Bauer's home to see the child, and he said that he was. He also said that he had called the paper to correct the statement that no physician had been called.

It was estimated by reporters that somewhere between 3,000 or 4,000 people were in that mob at its peak. Some were angry and involved, but most were simply there as sightseers. The huge crowd was easily equal to nearly one fourth to one fifth of the adult population of Mansfield. W. S. Cappeller, editor of the *Weekly News* suddenly realized what he had helped encourage and now the dumb ass reversed engine and wrote an editorial piece calling for calm, respect for rights, law and order. The paper also printed a message from Mayor Brown calling for keeping the peace and the dignity of the city.

While Fockler was being mobbed Mayor Brown was at a baseball game and, although notified what was going on, continued to enjoy the game but sent word to the leaders of the mob not to kill the Elder or hurt him seriously.

In an interview Fockler told a reporter that while he was being hustled down the street on a dead run towards the gas house there was one thing in his mind.

> Keep on your feet! Keep on your feet! If I had fallen down I would have been killed as the crowd would have trampled on me and kicked me to death. I kept my feet, offered no resistance and ran along with my captors.

Thousands of people were still mad as heck. They still wanted Fockler! That would not change.

Mansfield received a good bit of notoriety that it really didn't want. Newspapers around Ohio and elsewhere reported the affair. John Alexander Dowie, if he really didn't already know, had only to read the newspapers in his home base in Chicago.

Chicago Tribune, July 22, 1900 Dowie Elder Is Mobbed
Mansfield Police and Firemen Save Zion Leader

Mansfield O., (Special) Cyrus B. Fockler, Zion Elder, returned at noon on Saturday from Chicago by order of John Alexander Dowie and was mobbed by a crowd

of 5,000 citizens. He escaped the mob two weeks ago by leaving the city. Today Fockler was set upon and was faring badly when the whole police force of the city, aided by the fire department, succeeded in rescuing him. The firemen drenched the crowd with water while the officers used their clubs,...Fockler is alleged to have caused the death of children, estranged families, and driven several of his followers insane. He has also collected large sums of money from his Mansfield followers for Dowie, it is claimed. Some of his followers, it is claimed, have deeded their entire property over to him.

The details of the riot followed, though somewhat embellished. Most papers simply reported the riot while few editors condemned the actions. Several, with Zion problems in their own communities, felt that it may well have been justified.

A newspaper in Canton, Fockler's home town, had this to say:

Fig. 18. Mansfield's prison was a sad looking sandstone building on Walnut Street south of Park Avenue West, not far from the Square. A bewildered elder Fockler would have been only too happy to be safely inside its walls. (Phil Stoodt collection)

Canton News Democrat
July 23, 1900

The foreign missionary business got another jolt Saturday when it was again demonstrated that there is labor along mission lines to be performed at home. An order to bring all the missionaries of every denomination home from China and send them to Mansfield, Ohio, would be greatly appreciated. An occurrence there Saturday was a disgrace to the civilization of which Ohio boasts.

At the jail Fockler was examined by two doctors but refused to take any medicine though much pained in the abdomen. He ordered a new suit of clothes, sent a telegram to Dowie, and a conference was held with his lawyer and the mayor. It was decided to get the man out of town. It was Saturday night, and it was felt that if they waited the mob would be filled with liquor and in a "terrible condition."

Fig. 19. The Methodist Church on the Square, just across the street from the court house and only a few doors away from the Zion Tabernacle, was near the center of riot activity. (Richland County Chapter, Ohio Genealogical Society)

There was, however, a crowd still outside the jail. The escape was covered in the *Mansfield News*:

> **His escape from the city was arranged without further delay. The mayor drove up the alley at the south side of the jail with his two horses and a two seat open rig. Fockler came out through the coal hole in the cellar was hustled to the buggy by the police and the mayor whipped up his horses and the outfit drove through the crowd of spectators before the latter fully realized what had happened. Some of the crowd tried to stop the rig but did not succeed. In the buggy with the mayor were Attorney Douglass and Officer Goodman. The mayor drove to Ontario but when they reached that place they saw a big crowd around the town pump listening to one of its members reading from a Mansfield paper. They decided to take Fockler to Galion. It was his intention to take the Big Four train to Crestline from which place he could take an Erie train and return to Canton.**

Fig. 20. The E. L. Miller livery and cab service on North Walnut Street was one of many such businesses serving the horse and buggy trade in Mansfield. Automobiles were only a curiosity. It was a vulnerable way to move through the streets, especially through a wild mob. (Richland County Historical Society)

The clergy of Mansfield's churches found themselves on the spot as parishioners struggled with thoughts divided between drastic action and Christian forgiveness. Rev. E. F. Sherman of the Reformed Presbyterian church on Park Avenue West delivered a sermon on "Faith Cure for Children."

> **If it is not within the power of the authorities to protect infants from fatal neglect and acute suffering, it is time for more severe and definite legislation on the subject.**

His evening thought was "And the people stood beholding." One has to wonder if some Presbyterian with a wry sense of humor might have been the one holding Fockler's pants.

Dr. F. A. Gould of the First Methodist Episcopal Church titled his two sermons, "Satisfaction doing God's work and will," and in the evening "Mob law in Mansfield." In part of his remarks, which were reprinted in the paper, he said,

> **To charge the responsibility for the action of the mob to the press and pulpit of Mansfield is not right. It is not the Mansfield press, it is not the pulpit, nor the officers of Mansfield who should be held responsible for the work of the mob on that day. Lots of people in that crowd were farmers and others drawn thither by curiosity.... Mr. Fockler has been here for months abusing the churches, the pulpit, the physicians, the city officials, the Y.M.C.A and even the Salvation Army came in for its share of**

vituperation. The paper Leaves of Healing with its abuse and vile language was distributed and stirred up sentiment . . . . If that paper represents Dr. Dowie and his movement; if that is the spirit of Christ—God help us.

Though not always recorded in the Mansfield newspapers, there is evidence that nearly all Protestant and Catholic congregations would wrestle with what course of conduct they should follow. Their choices ranged from condemnation to forgiveness or simply remaining silent and looking away. The eyes of God and the country were on them all. It must have been an uncomfortable time for many.

William Lawrence, editor of the *Mansfield Daily Shield*, again stirring the pot, printed a letter from a "reliable person" in Chicago who had attended Dowie's service in Zion Tabernacle the previous Sunday July 15. Parts of it are as follows.

> The principal of the "Doctor's" (Dowie) prayer was, "O Lord, smite that miserable Mayor Brown of Mansfield, and smite him quick." His followers to the number of 2,000 responded with a loud "Amen."

> After the prayer he devoted two hours to a discussion of the crisis in Mansfield . . . . He characterized the Board of Health of Mansfield as the "Board of Death" and the town itself as "Devils Field." He said, "Mayor Brown, don't imagine you can fight Zion. Zion will light a fire under you. Whoever touches Zion will be hurt. You are an enemy of righteousness. You are not ready for the trial of Fockler and you won't be ready for the trial of the great white throne. You are an unclean dog and will die the death of a dog and that is an insult to the dog."

Dowie then announced that he was sending Fockler and three other elders to hold services in Mansfield next Sunday. He said that if they were harmed in any way he would follow in person on Monday with 300 Zion guards and train loads of Dowieites from Chicago, Cincinnati, Cleveland, Lima, Ada and take the town. The nit-wit editor of the paper ended the column with this sentence:

> The above letter is given to the public this afternoon and its contents will no doubt create a sensation.

It did!

A telegram was received at police headquarters directed to Mayor Brown:

> Rev E. P. Fisher, Evangelist in charge of Zion Tabernacle in Mansfield, informs me there is danger of mob violence tonight. I demand his protection by authorities. We shall never yield to mob law. He will stay and minister to the members of his church in Mansfield come what will. Your duty is to protect him at all risks.
>
> **John Alex. Dowie**

Shortly after Chief Clark had received this message, the mayor being absent, Fisher, the Evangelist, walked into police headquarters. He came in unannounced and appeared as though he had dropped down from the sky, when it was thought he had left the city for a few days.

Chief Clark informed Fisher that he was in danger of being mobbed and advised him to leave town. The Elder resisted and moved around town trying to rent a hall for services on Sunday. A rumor was started by one of his Zion flock to the effect that Dowie would send a woman Elder to the Mansfield congregation with the idea that a woman wouldn't be mistreated or mobbed.

Sheriff Pulver received two telegrams, one on July 27, from Dowie and later one from Ohio Governor George K. Nash.

When Fockler was being roughed up he lost his notebook and other personal items. The notebook was given to a reporter who dutifully printed the names and addresses of all 15 Zion members listed inside and noted Fockler had $500 in Richland Bank. It was then turned over to Mayor Brown who returned it to Fockler.

Sunday July 29 passed rather peacefully. A period of contemplation had set in. The CCC church held their services in the Zion tabernacle on Park Avenue East while police and Sheriff Pulver stood by. There was a small crowd outside but no trouble.

William Hamner Piper, General Overseer at Large of Zion, John Alexander Dowie's well-dressed number two man, had been dispatched from Chicago to put out the fires in "Devils Field." With him were Elders Mc Clurkin, Stevens, Kennedy, McFarland and Evangelist Fisher. Perhaps it was felt that there was strength in numbers, which proved to be the case. They were met at the depot by Sheriff Pulver and taken in a cab to the Vonhof Hotel where they were assigned rooms 42, 53 and 54. An eager beaver reporter printed the rumor that two members of the party were Pinkerton detectives armed with rifles and revolvers. He could get the facts later!

Through lawyer Douglass, a restraining order issued by the court had temporarily returned the use of the unfinished Laver building to the Dowie congregation after no other place in town could be rented. The seating consisted of rough boards laid across chairs. Overseer Piper would later comment that if a man had a beef steak in front of him it wouldn't matter what he was sitting on.

During the evening five large boxes arrived at the tabernacle and immediately the rumor spread that they contained firearms and ammunition. An excited group of young men demanded that they be opened and under police supervision church members pried them open. Inside were several thousand copies of *Leaves of Healing*.

Fig. 21. Willam Hammer Piper was the number two man in the Dowie church. He came to Mansfield with five elders in an effort to defuse the situation. (Zion Historical Society)

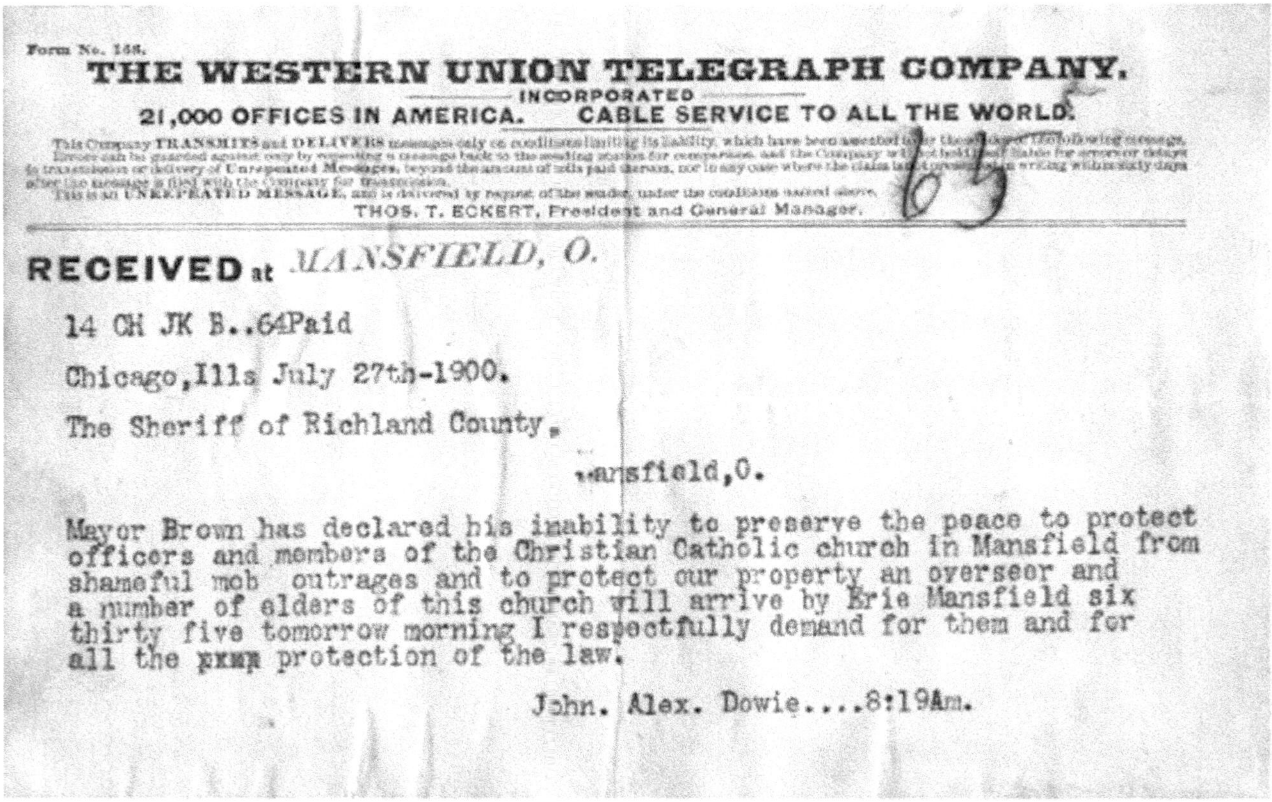

Form No. 168.

THE WESTERN UNION TELEGRAPH COMPANY.
INCORPORATED
21,000 OFFICES IN AMERICA. CABLE SERVICE TO ALL THE WORLD.

This Company TRANSMITS and DELIVERS messages only on conditions limiting its liability, which have been assented to by the sender of the following message.
Errors can be guarded against only by repeating a message back to the sending station for comparison, and the Company will not hold itself liable for errors or delays in transmission or delivery of Unrepeated Messages, beyond the amount of tolls paid thereon, nor in any case where the claim is not presented in writing within sixty days after the message is filed with the Company for transmission.
This is an UNREPEATED MESSAGE, and is delivered by request of the sender, under the conditions named above.
THOS. T. ECKERT, President and General Manager.

RECEIVED at MANSFIELD, O.

14 CH JK B..64Paid

Chicago, Ills July 27th-1900.

The Sheriff of Richland County,

Mansfield, O.

Mayor Brown has declared his inability to preserve the peace to protect officers and members of the Christian Catholic church in Mansfield from shameful mob outrages and to protect our property an overseer and a number of elders of this church will arrive by Erie Mansfield six thirty five tomorrow morning I respectfully demand for them and for all the xxxx protection of the law.

John. Alex. Dowie....8:19Am.

Figs. 22 and 23. Sheriff Pulver received two telegrams, one from John Alexander Dowie and another from Ohio Governor George K. Nash. (Pulver Scrapbook, Robert Carter collection)

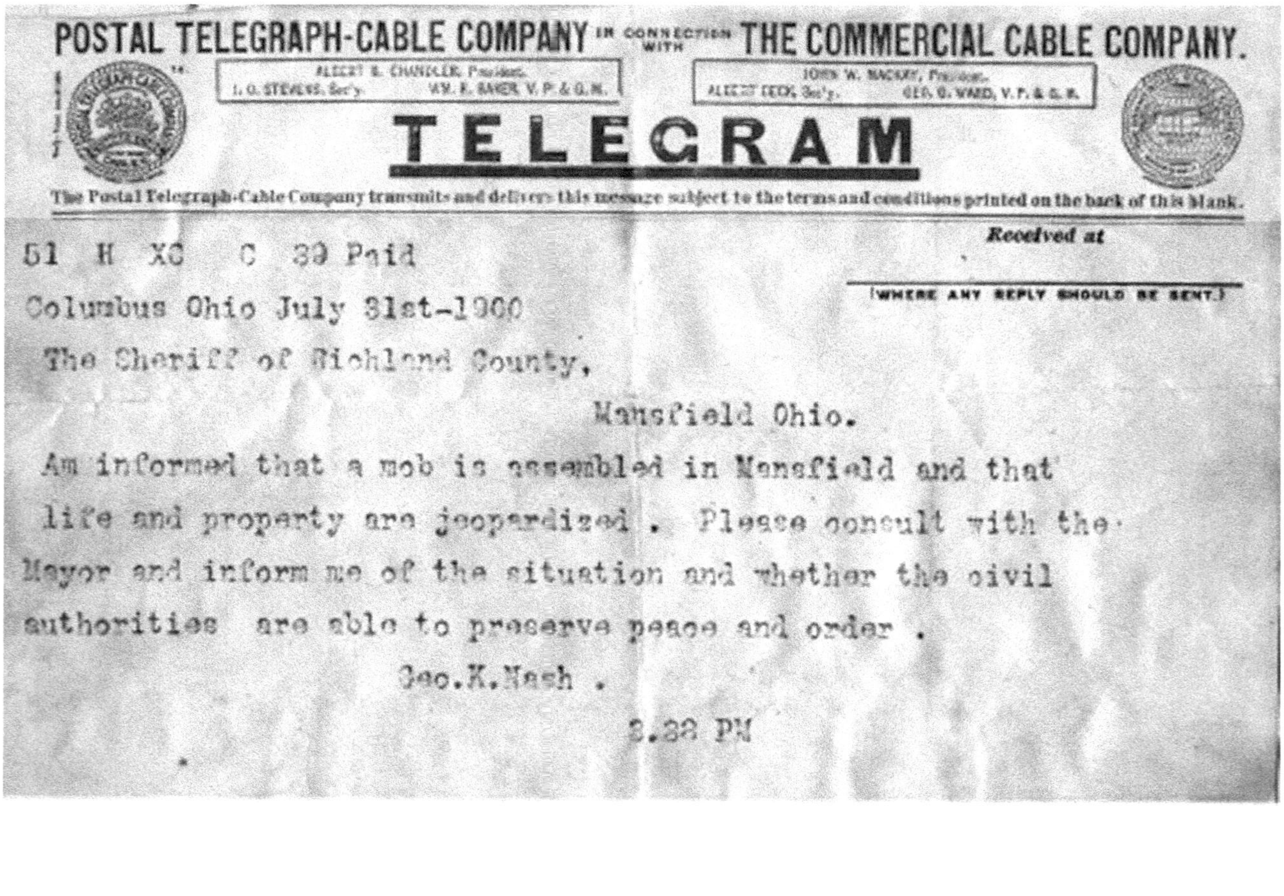

POSTAL TELEGRAPH-CABLE COMPANY IN CONNECTION WITH THE COMMERCIAL CABLE COMPANY.

TELEGRAM

The Postal Telegraph-Cable Company transmits and delivers this message subject to the terms and conditions printed on the back of this blank.

51 H XC C 39 Paid

Columbus Ohio July 31st-1900

The Sheriff of Richland County,

Mansfield Ohio.

Am informed that a mob is assembled in Mansfield and that life and property are jeopardized. Please consult with the Mayor and inform me of the situation and whether the civil authorities are able to preserve peace and order.

Geo. K. Nash.

3.22 PM

Having been warned by Sheriff Pulver, Mayor Brown and the lawyers not to cause trouble, Piper delivered the morning message to a crowd of about 150. Only about 70 were CCC members, the rest being curious visitors. His sermon entitled "Shall we trust God or Physicians" was conciliatory.

> **There is no man Zion has intentionally injured in any way. We have come to preach the gospel of the kingdom of God. We come with no hatred to anyone. There is no man Zion has intentionally injured in any way. We have come to Mansfield to preach the gospel of the kingdom of God. We come with no hatred to anyone. I love all men, even my enemies . . . . Is medicine a science? Why then does a physician guess so often? We know the names of the leaders of the mob. If a physician got a coat of tar and feathers for every babe that died under his ministrations he'd have a number of coats. Unfortunately one of the members of this church went insane. If elder Fockler should be mobbed for this why should not the Methodist minister be mobbed? Neither is right. The devil is responsible for it. Mob the devil by giving up your wicked habits. I came here to rob the devil.**

His sermon continued to abuse the schools of allopathic and homeopathic medicine. He also stated that he knew the names of the leaders of the mob and said they were at his mercy. After the service was over, the crowd filed quietly out and a short time later the Dowie group made their way back to the hotel unmolested.

Piper also preached the afternoon service to a smaller crowd during which time several young men removed their jackets due to the heat and a heavy summer downpour outside. Piper requested that they put them back on. They left, as did a small crowd gathered outside. Piper, noticing the heavy rain, remarked that "the fire company would not need their hose this afternoon." During the service he said:

Fig. 24. Dowie printed his own newspaper in an attempt to counter the negative coverage he received in the American press. (Huntington Brown Scrapbook, Sherman Room collection, M/RCPL)

Fig. 25. Dowie's church newspaper Leaves of Healing vilified Mansfield authorities cartoon-style and condemned their actions. (Huntington Brown scrapbook, Sherman Room collection, M/RCPL)

It was alright for members to seek the assistance of a physician and take medicine if they chose to do so. He said to quit sinning and lead righteous lives were a requirement for admission to and continuance in the Christian Catholic Church and that those who did not pay their debts and treat their fellow man right could not retain membership.

This was evidently an effort to smooth over the strict dictates Fockler preached. Prayed for were the city officials and mob leaders whose names Piper knew including one "poor, misguided "Red" Hartman, the leader of the mob." He also pronounced John Alexander Dowie "the mightiest man that has lived since the apostle Paul."

Although Overseer Piper and Evangelist Fisher had arrived from Chicago to take over for Fockler in order to allay local hostilities, unfortunately the other arrival from Chicago—the crates of church propaganda—had the opposite effect.

Chapter 3
Another Outbreak of Mob Violence

Sunday passed peacefully and no mutterings of discontent were heard until Monday. Then things started to get ugly. A small crowd of men gathered at the square in the evening and it was learned that the Zion Elders would be preaching at the home of Mrs. Lidia C. Frederick at 16 Wayne Street. Bent on interrupting the services the group increased in size as it wound its way north from the square down to Wayne Street. By the time they reached their destination it had become an angry mob with people lining both sides of the street.

What happened next was covered by a reporter on the scene. His words, reprinted here, beautifully detail the mob action as they appeared in the July 31, 1900, *Mansfield Daily Shield*.

ELDER A. McFARLANE.   ELDER GERALD F. STEVENS.
ELDER A. W. McCLURKIN.   EVANGELIST E. P. FISHER.

Fig. 26. The four Zion preachers sent to Mansfield were attacked by an angry mob: two roughed up, two painted blue, and all four jailed for their protection. (Zion Historical Society)

The Zion flock to the number of 40 or 50 were gathered in the parlor of the Frederick house and the services were conducted by Elders McClurkin, Stevens, McFarland and Evangelist Fisher.

In a short time the members of the mob appeared at the house and demanded Fisher. The Zion Elders barricaded the doors and sent some frightened women upstairs. Soon the trouble began. Someone in the crowd threw a rock through one of the windows and the trouble was on. The Zion elders returned the rock through the windows and injured three or four young men who had approached the house for the purpose of taking the women to a place of safety. This incensed the mob and the rear door was battered down. The situation indeed looked critical!

Authorities Arrive

Chief Clark, Sheriff "Barney" Pulver, Deputy Tom Bell and several police officers appeared on the scene and made a stand on the front porch of the besieged house. The crowd, however, could not be cheated of its objective and crowded its way up to the porch with wild yells. Sheriff Pulver commanded the mob to disperse in the name of the law but it had no effect on the determined mob. The police offered to take the Zion ministers to the jail for safe keeping but the mob would not listen to it. Before the police arrived the Zion elders fought desperately in the sitting room of the house which was soon demolished. Inflammable waste material was thrown into the rooms where the Zion ministers fought desperately. A number of threats were made to dynamite the building.

Soon the mob gained entrance to the house by means of the rear door. The crowd jostled their way past the authorities like an avalanche and poured upstairs where Fisher and McClurkin were in hiding. The two were dragged downstairs and out into the yard through the rear entrance into the hands of the relentless mob. The two elders, McFarland and Stevens took refuge with the women and children in the sitting room and the entrance was barred by Sheriff Pulver and the police. Sheriff Pulver, while the mob was surging around him, intent on gaining possession of the elders, strongly considered the advisability of asking aid from Governor Nash.

The frightened women and children were huddled together for safety by the mob and were led out of the building one by one in a hysterical condition, some went

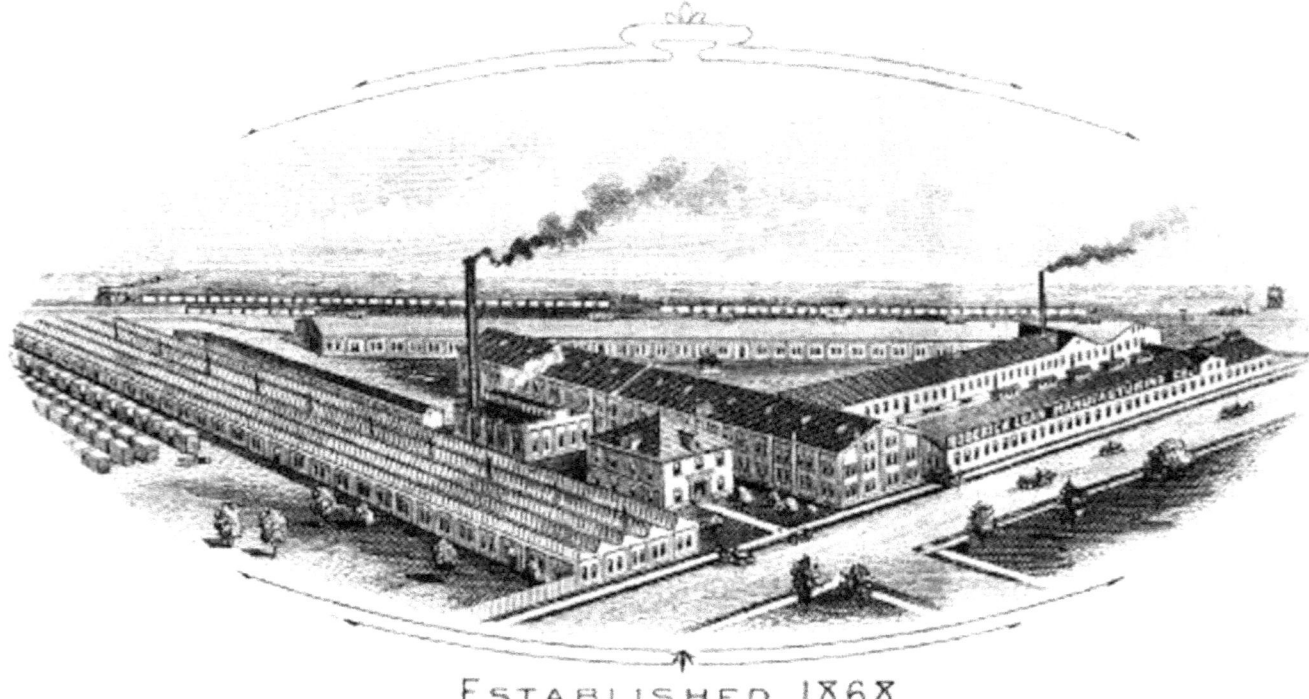

Fig. 27. The Roderick Lean Harrow Works was just east of the railroad tracks on the road to Wooster. It was one of the largest manufacturiong plants in Mansfield employing many hands. Some employees evidently helped the mob that painted the Elders. (Phil Stoodt collection)

unwillingly. The elders McFarland and Stevens remained in the building but were badly frightened. They consented to leave Mansfield for the present if they should be taken to city prison for safety. The mob cried loudly for Fisher but it became known that he was not in the house. While authorities were busy protecting McFarland and Stevens in the parlor, Fisher and McClurkin had been dragged downstairs and away before the authorities and half the mob was aware of it.

The mob which was dispersing rapidly, agreed not to molest Elders Stevens and McFarland and on the strength of this Sheriff Pulver and Deputy Bell escorted the two men towards the city prison. A majority of the mob, hearing cheering in the direction of the Lean Harrow Works hurried to that place.

Elders McGlurkin and Fisher had been hustled through the alley at the rear where the crowd halted as the leaders deliberated and determined a course of action. It was the will of the crowd that they be treated the same as Fockler and was suggested they proceed to the gas house, but the fact that Fockler's dose was not as successful as had been expected the idea was abandoned. Before many minutes had lapsed the two Zionites were being hurried away in the direction of the Lean Harrow Works, where their clothes, with the exception of their coats and vests which were removed with some degree of carefulness, were fairly torn from their bodies by the impatient mob, many enthusiast securing fragments of the torn garments as souvenirs.

Fig. 28. The blue Elders nearly ended up in the Central Park fountain, but the mob, who had nearly killed the men, didn't want to endanger the goldfish. (Richland County Historical Society)

Then took place a sight that would have made Dowie himself, laugh at the sheer ridiculousness of the scene. The victims were seized by the leaders and literally painted blue from head to foot!

The paint which is used for painting harrows and which was secured after defying the watchman, was applied with brooms and with their bodies having been thoroughly saturated with royal blue the baptism was made complete by dousing a full bucket of the ingredients over each.

The elders were taken for a stroll with an occasional spin. It was suggested at the Park Avenue railroad crossing that they be taken to the ice pond for another immersion, but better counsel prevailed with the mob which at any time could not be considered turbulent or bloodthirsty, and the two elders of Zion, shining like newly varnished Lean harrows were made to proceed ahead of the mob up Park Avenue East to Central Park. Numerous threats were made to throw them into the fountain, but owing to the suggestion that they might kill the fish, they were spared the ordeal. They were then taken to their destination, the police station.

Several officers and Sheriff Pulver arrived at the city jail with Elder Stevens of Chicago and McFarland of Marion only a few minutes before the crowd made its appearance and delivered the blue coated forms of Fisher and McGlurkin. Olin Faber, who had urged the crowd at the Lean Harrow Works to take the elders to city prison, took the steps and immediately his name was called. He said the crowd had accomplished its purpose and it was now time to disperse and return to their homes. Mayor Brown opened the door of the prison and as he did, Faber suggested three cheers for the mayor, and the crowd responded with three ringing cheers which awakened the west end residents.

Mayor Brown then asked the crowd to disperse. "This is unlawful," he said. "Let the law take its course. All go quietly to your homes." Content with what it had done, the crowd began to leave the prison and in a short while the streets were practically deserted.

The *Mansfield News* reported that when the elders were marched up Park Avenue East the crowd wanted to lock them inside their tabernacle and keep them there until morning. This would allow their paint time to dry. Others wanted them to get up on a high platform outside and deliver a speech or preach a sermon. The newspaper also added this:

They were hustled up and down the steps in front of the building and made very grotesque figures in the electric light, their skin shining like looking glasses with the coats of blue paint. It was a sight that will linger in the minds of those who saw it for many a day. Here Mr. Faber again got the crowd's attention for a moment, reminded them that it was getting late and that everyone had enough fun for one night. He finally persuaded the crowd to move again.

It was nearly midnight when the painted elders were safe behind bars and the cleanup begun. Their hair, beards and bodies seemed to gleam with the royal blue from the Lean Harrow works, nice and shiny like a new farm implement. Rags were first tried to remove the now sticky drying paint but the material stuck making things worse and with their blue hair and beards became a laughable sight. A doctor was called and ordered large quantity of Vaseline be rubbed over their bodies and then coal oil was applied followed by lard and then more coal oil. It had to have been one hell of a mess!

The writer's grandmother, Mary Pulver Carter, was the oldest daughter of Sheriff Pulver. She was 18 at the time and as was the custom in that era, the sheriff and his family lived in the family quarters of the Richland County Jail. She used to help her mother cook and feed the prisoners. Mary often told her father's story of cleaning the painted Dowies.

When it was time to scrub the paint off there was a black man in jail for some offence and he was ordered to help scrub the royal blue off the elders. After all, neither the mayor, the sheriff or the police wanted that blue mess on their clothing. The prisoner refused, saying he would do almost anything but there was no way he was going to wash a white man. At that point he was informed there would be nothing for him to eat until the blue men were cleaned up. A wash tub was brought in and the prisoner laid into the two elders with a stiff scrub brush and the yells of pain could be heard outside in the street.

After the paint was off they were given a bath and a new suit of clothes was ordered for each. Then a carriage arrived and the four were driven to the county jail where Elder McFarland sent the following telegram to William Hamner Piper in Chicago, the General Overseer at Large of the CCC:

> **Evangelist Fisher and Elder McClurkin were captured by a mob and painted. We are now in prison safe**
>
> **Signed, A. W. McFarland.**

Dowie and Piper had already received an earlier telegram from Mansfield. After the mob delivered two of the Zion leaders to the jail some jokesters sent this to Dowie:

> **Dr. Alex. Dowie, Chicago:**
>
> **Elder Fisher and his mate have been nicely painted blue. The police were so busy looking for the nut spielers attached with the Nickel Plate Show hence the elders were nicely daubed with the otter marine blue. Waiting for more elders.**
>
> **Signed Mansfield Blues**

Sheriff Pulver was not in a good mood. During the fracas on the Frederick porch he had been mistaken by some in the crowd as a Dowie elder. During the tussle to take him off the porch he lost his cuff buttons and suspenders. One wonders if he had to walk back uptown to the jail holding up his pants with one hand and the Dowies with the other.

The Frederick house had been heavily damaged and later a photograph of it would appear in an issue of *Leaves of Healing*.

The following day, Tuesday, July 31, 1900, the *Mansfield Shield & Banner* under a headline

Fig. 29. Mary Pulver, (front row left) the oldest daughter of Sheriff "Barney" Pulver, lived at the jail and kept a scrapbook of her father's time in office. In her later years she and her husband George Carter recalled what they knew. George told how he started to follow a mob when the family doctor grabbed him by the arm and told him not to go. "Your father wouldn't approve," he said. (Robert Carter collection)

"Again The Mob Breaks Loose" started their page with a long condemnation of Monday's violence :

> The "Shield" has no words of defense to utter on behalf of the mob. Its performance last night was like that of nearly all mobs—it was irrational, inhumane and cowardly. For a hundred men to maltreat two men is not a brave thing to do. For a mob to persecute and abuse a few non-resisting persons, making the tax payers liable for heavy damages, is destitute of business sense as well as common humanity . . . . This exhibition of mobocracy has seldom been equaled in the State of Ohio. There have been a number of instances of lynching and mob violence in which the victims were either killed or lost their lives but there have been few instances where men were painted, tarred and feathered and then turned over to authorities in an orderly manner.

Fig. 30. This photograph from Leaves of Healing shows damage done to the Frederick house. The door is unhinged and windows broken with trash littering the floor. Though only one room is depicted, the entire house suffered damage. This house on Newman Street is no longer in existence, having been replaced by a factory building in the 1920s. (Zion Historical Society)

> # MANSFIELD SHIELD EXTRA.
>
> THIRTEENTH YEAR, NO. 87.   MANSFIELD, OHIO, TUESDAY EVENING, JULY 31, 1900.
>
> ## AGAIN THE MOB BREAKS LOOSE!
>
> ### Another Terrible Night of Fever and Turmoil in Mansfield. Citizens Arise in Their Wrath.
>
> ### TWO ZION MINISTERS STRIPPED AND PAINTED.
>
> Their Boardinghouse Wrecked by Indignant and Enraged Citizens—The Distribution Throughout the City of "The Leaves of Healing," the Official Organ of Dowie, Containing Calumnious and Scurrilous Attacks on Mansfield and its Citizens, Created Intense Indignation and Incited the Citizens to Mob Violence.

Fig. 31. The front page of Mansfield's newspapers was ordinarily covered with stories from across the United States or around the world. Rarely did local news make it to the front page as it did on July 21 when the entire top half of the page above the fold was covered in bold type. (Sherman Room microfilm, M/RCPL)

After those remarks, the editor carried a reporter's complete blow-by-blow account of the whole mob riot. The newspaper's attitude continued to flip-flop from day to day, story by story. After previously praising efforts by the sheriff and police in saving Fockler and attempts to maintain order the idiot editor had this to say on Wednesday after the affair, a riot for which his paper was in no small part responsible:

> **How humiliating it is for the citizens of Mansfield to learn that Governor Nash was on the very point of sending two companies of National Guard to our city to crush our lawlessness and control the mob before our legal officers cowered and fled. A half-dozen excitable men did all the damage. The right kind of peace officer could have stopped this lawlessness in its incipiency. But the peace officers showed the white feather and surrendered to the noisy rioters—what could be expected? What a humiliating, pitiable sight it was to see the mayor of Mansfield, with the law on his side and the whole state of Ohio at his back, begging a small gathering at the railroad station to permit him to send men out of town—men that had never committed any crime as far as we know.**

Evidently Editor Lawrence of the *Democratic Shield & Banner* stayed behind or hid under his desk during the whole affair. He had no explanation of how just a few police officers were to control a mob numbering in the hundreds or perhaps a thousand or more. His remarks also took a swipe at the Republican Mayor Brown and his administration. Surprisingly, due to overwhelming public sentiment against the Dowies, both newspapers (*Democrat Shield & Banner* and *Republican Mansfield News*) had generally supported the elected officials rather than the usual partisan bickering.

A conference was held the next morning in Sheriff Pulver's office at the county jail. Present were the four Zion ministers, Mayor Brown, Deputy Bell, Chief of Police Clark, Prosecuting Attorney Bowers, Attorneys A. A. Douglass and James Seward, a few prominent business leaders and others including two reporters. The Dowies were greatly encouraged to leave the city and protection would be offered. They responded by saying they had been ordered here through Overseer Piper on orders from John Alexander Dowie and could not leave unless they were given permission to do so. A long-distance phone call was placed to Chicago and the situation was explained to Piper by Attorney Douglass and the elders. Attorney Douglass said 250 men armed to the teeth could not cope with the mob. Dowie was "across the lake at his summer residence" and Piper reluctantly gave in and wired them $100 for clothing and train fare. It wasn't quite enough.

As reported in the *Shield,* Mansfield and the darned farmers gave them a send-off:

> **When four cabs drew up at 11:45 on the driveway at the county jail a large crowd began to gather to watch the ministers depart. The Chief of Police and Officer Madden were in the carriage with Fisher and Stevens and Capt. Crider was in the carriage with the other two. The ministers were short of money and $40 was loaned to them. The Pennsylvania ticket office was notified that the men were coming and that tickets should be ready for them and the start was made. The cabs went down Diamond Street at a rapid rate. The Sheriff, deputy, mayor, Attorneys Seward and Douglass as well as members of the police force went in the other carriages to the depot. Crowds began to run towards the Union Depot and as the station was reached, crowds of men were seen running from every direction towards the platform. Men, women and children swelled the crowd which filled the platform from the depot to the telegraph office and extended upon the tracks. The men swarmed around the carriages containing the Dowies but no attempt was made to molest them. Fisher and Stevens went into the depot for the tickets.**
>
> **Mayor Brown speaks**
>
> **Mayor Brown delivered a short address from the driver's seat of one of the cabs. It was brief but to the point. "I ask, I beseech of you, people that you refrain from any attempt whatsoever to molest these people, but allow them to go in peace. I ask that you shall in no manner molest them. Will you do this?**
>
> **"Yes," was the reply from the multitude as if of one man. Let them go away. Three cheers were given for the mayor.**

The west bound Pennsylvania, Ft. Wayne & Chicago 12:05 arrived and the four men were escorted through the crowd by Sheriff Pulver and police officers and remained on board with them until the train started. A loud long cheer went up as they left.

It seemed rather suspicious that the elders who had been taken away were painted so quickly. A reporter went to the Lean Harrow Works and asked the night watchman if he had recognized anyone or if any members of the mob were employees of the firm. He replied, "No sir, some of them were from New York but the majority was from Chicago."

Well, so much for that investigation.

John Alexander Dowie was hopping mad as one might expect. There had been protests and mob actions against his Zion Church in other cities but nothing as violent as what had happened in Mansfield. The story made newspapers all across the United States. He sent telegrams to Sheriff Pulver, Mayor Brown and appealed to Ohio Governor George Nash to send troops from the National Guard. He even sent a telegram to President McKinley, who was vacationing in Canton. Dowie had to stop this violence before other cities tried to copy Mansfield. He condemned what had happened to his Elders and very strongly criticized local police and elected officials for not protecting his flock. He threatened to send "a train load of Zion guards" to Mansfield which prompted Governor Nash to comment that they would never cross the state line, and if they did they would be met by 10,000 Ohio National Guards.

Fig. 32. Mansfield attorney A. A. Douglass was hired to represent Fockler and the Dowie preachers. He was strongly condemned and sometimes threatened for his defense of the Zion members. (Sherman Room collection, M/RCPL)

Storming mad in Chicago, Dowie had this to say to his followers about the nation's President:

> **They call this a land of liberty, civil and religious, where every man can worship God according to the dictates of his own conscience. Why did not President McKinley prevent it? He was only 60 miles away in Canton, and yet he did not make a move in our behalf. Think of that! A Republican President, whom Zion helped elect four years ago—and we did help to elect him too, for he personally thanked me for the votes I brought him from Zion: this Republican President did not raise a finger to help us in our distress. I and Zion were with him four years ago but if he does not get a move on and do something we'll be against him this fall.**

Sheriff Pulver and Mayor Brown received and sent quite a few telegrams and the Western Union Telegraph Company office must have been a busy place. Telegrams, from newspapers all around the country wanting information on the troubles, came like an avalanche.

There were many eyes watching the railroad stations and any new arrivals in town. Two well-dressed strangers appeared at the Vonhof Hotel and one tried to arrange for a room. The second conferred with him a few minutes while a few men bystanders watched. Refused a room the two started up the street towards the Brunswick Hotel. Suspicions

Fig. 33. The Union Station served both the Erie Railroad and the Pittsburgh, Fort Wayne & Chicago (often called Pennsylvania) passengers. It was located off of North Diamond Street where the two lines crossed. (Mansfield Memorial Museum)

arose that they were Dowie elders and a few more men followed them. Others quickly joined in the march which soon increased in size to several hundred. Along the way a meeting of the Catholic Knights had just let out and they joined in but someone finally suggested that they ascertain the identity of the two strangers. After explaining and showing papers, Catholic Priest Father Lasoski and Chicago real estate salesman L.W. Pociechoski identified themselves. Both men were on their way to Canton to see President McKinley and help round up some Polish Republican voters in New York and New Jersey. The red-faced crowd quickly melted away.

A policeman then escorted the two to the Tremont House near the railroad station. The difference between the Vonhof, where they were refused a room, and the Tremont is comparable to a four star Hilton verses a Motel 6. The saloons and brothels were between the station and the upper part of town. The two travelers were very unhappy about their treatment.

Another small embarrassment was reprinted locally from the *Chicago Chronicle*:

> **John Alexander Dowie continues to enjoy good luck. He has been favored by fortune—Providence, he would probably call it—for the last seven years. His enemies continue to advertise him free of charge.**

> **Just now it is the citizens of Mansfield, O., who are doing promotion and publicity work for Zion. They have mobbed two of Dowie's missionaries and thereby attracted**

the attention of the State of Ohio to the Dowie cult. At regular advertising rates it would have cost $25,000 to achieve the wide publicity which has thus been furnished absolutely free of charge.

A meeting was held by Mayor Brown, and a consultation was held with his attorneys and a number of citizens representing both political parties, including former Democratic mayor Robert C. McCrory (Brown was a Republican.) They read an opinion from Ohio Attorney General Sheets who wrote the following; "In my opinion they were guilty of provoking a breach of the peace and were clearly guilty of criminal libel against the mayor of your city. And I think now as I have examined a copy of *Leaves of Healing* and when those elders came to the city and circulated the *Leaves of Healing* they were clearly guilty of criminal libel, and if they insist on coming back, I think the thing to do is arrest them before people get excited and organize another mob."

After a long deliberation a course of action was decided by Mayor Brown. He ordered that if any Zion Elders return they would be escorted out of the city in the interest of law and order.

And so that was the word. If they come in, we'll throw them out!

It was a tough decision. Under Ohio law "Any person assaulted by a mob or suffering lynching at their hands, shall be entitled to recover of the county in which such assault was made, the sum of $500; or if the injury received is serious the sum of $1,000; or if it results in permanent disability to earn a living by manual labor, the sum of $5,000." And then there were possible damages and court costs.

Fig. 34. The B&O depot, another scene of several mob events during the summer of 1900, was located on Mulberry Street, just west of the Union Station. (Phil Stoodt collection)

Fig. 35. President William McKinley and Governor Nash as depicted in the columns of the <u>Mansfield News</u>. (Sherman Room microfilm, M/RCPL)

Fig. 36. This photograph from 1898 depicts a crowd at the B&O station awaiting troop trains for the Spanish American War. Although not a scene from the Dowie protests in 1900, it illustrates was the Zion Elders must have seen as they entered or departed Mansfield. (Sherman Room collection, M/RCPL)

Mansfield News, August 2

There was something of a sensation when train No. 20 on the P. F. pulled into the depot at 8:45 p.m. At least 1,000 to 1,200 people were there. The people were packed so closely on the platform that it was with difficulty that passengers were able to dismount from the train. There was only one man on the train that wore whiskers and a long coat and he was given pretty close scrutiny by a self appointed committee of a whole. Some of the crowd went on the train and talked with a stranger who looked like a Zionite and he was greatly amused by the incident. Another big crowd went to the B&O depot and met the train from Chicago last night at 9:30. No elders came over that route and the authorities were again agreeably disappointed.

The police and about 125 people met the Chicago and New York Flyer on the P.F. at 12:20. It is stated that the authorities will not depart from their determination to fire all elders and the people themselves are there to see that it is done.

And in the same column was this:

It was reported last night that a number of girls who are employed in the cigar factories held a meeting and decided to give a female elder, who came the day before the two elders were painted, notice to leave the city. A number of additional letters and post cards have gone forth to Dowie and Piper at Chicago, warning them not to send any more elders of either sex to Mansfield unless they wanted to see them painted and sent back to Chicago in a sealed box car.

Fig. 37. The Tremont House hotel and restaurant was located across from the railroad station. It was low cost but noisy due to the nearly continual train traffic. It is doubtful that the two Polish Republicans slept well. (Phil Stoodt collection)

MAYOR BROWN--ANY PLACE BUT HERE.

Fig. 38. Mayor Brown, the police, and Sheriff Pulver made regular trips to the railroad depots escorting Dowie preachers out of town. The News cartoon told the story. (Sherman Room microfilm, M/RCPL)

On Wednesday evening August 1, a group of about 40 married and unmarried women met at a secret rendezvous with secret pass words and hatched a plan to tar and feather the woman Zion preacher who was rumored to be in the city. About 300 women had agreed to par ticipate but a rumor that the woman had left town kept the group smaller than planned. About 8 o'clock they started for the suspected home where the preacher was supposed to be but arriving, but were refused entrance being told the woman was not there. A delegation was allowed in and searched the house anyway. As reported in the *Mansfield Shield and Banner*:

The crowd of disappointed women which made a search for the woman stated that the reason for the action last night was because the woman had said

> that she could preach as much as she pleased in Mansfield and that she would not be molested by a mob of men. It seems she had not taken the women into account. A young woman who was in the crowd refused to tell where they had started from but said it was not far from the Zion tabernacle.

There is no record but one could only guess that word of the female mob might have caused Mayor Brown to lean back in his chair and stare at the ceiling. Sheriff Pulver's forehead may have hit his desk. What officer of the law in his right mind would want to try to corral a mob of angry determined women?

The next day Sheriff *Barney* Pulver received a telegram from old Dowie himself.

With the impending *invasion* coming what might be called a war council was held in the circuit court room. The telegram from Dowie was read and Congressman W. S. Kerr was appointed chairman and T. F. Black secretary. Assembled were the mayor, sheriff, police officials, Judge Wolfe, a minister and an assortment of lawyers, business leaders and citizens.

It was found that Dowie and Piper had notified newspapers in Columbus, Cincinnati, Chicago and other places of their intention to arrive on Sunday, thus advertising the coming conflict. Governor Nash sent a long letter which said, in effect, if you can't keep the peace or can't handle it, call me. He ignored Dowie's plea for the Ohio National Guard troops. Unknown was how some members of the guard would react or could be trusted if they did come. It was suggested the trains be boarded at Galion or Crestline and never let them get to Mansfield. A long message was sent to Dowie and Piper telling them and their people to stay away for a while until things cooled down. It wasn't safe for them to come to Mansfield. Their advice was ignored.

Figs. 39 and 40. Many young women worked in Mansfield industries. The cigar factories, suspender plants and the Crawford Steam Cracker works were just three. (Leftt, Robert Carter collection, right, Mark Hertzler collection)

The *Ohio State Journal*, Columbus August 1.

There is trouble in Zion. John Alexander Dowie on Tuesday telegraphed Governor Nash, demanding for the representatives of his sect the immediate protection of the state against the mob which tarred and feathered two of the brethren at Mansfield, Monday night. Mr. Dowie telegraphed from Montague, Mich., and his first telegraph was received at 1:18 pm. Half an hour later another telegram more urgent came from him.

The Governor, after writing the sheriff of Richland County, at Mansfield, for advice as to the exact situation , sent John Alexander a little information concerning the chief executives duty in time of such stress and a little advice to the propriety of tempering ones zeal. He said:

"When civil authorities of Mansfield and Richland County inform me that they are unable to preserve the peace and protect life and property, it will be time for me to act. In the meantime it would be well for you to temper you zeal with some degree of prudence."

Local preparations went forward. A number of special policemen were sworn in by the mayor. Sheriff Pulver had thirty deputies sworn in by the County Clerk. The fire department would be on hand if needed. Adjutant General of Ohio George Gyger and his assistant came from Columbus to keep the Governor advised and call the Ohio National Guard if necessary. A meeting was held in Prosecutor Bowers office at 10:00 o'clock with General Geyger, Judge Wolfe, Mayor Brown, Editor Cappeller and Judge Brucker. Also present were John Rapier, assistant editor of the *Cleveland Press*, Franklin Hall of the *Cleveland Plain Dealer,* and Arthur Kessling of the *Cincinnati Post*.

A special grand jury had been impaneled to examine charges to be brought against both the Zion elders and the leaders of the mobs. This was a significant effort to get a handle on the whole embarrassing situation. Warrants and arrests would follow.

Good God, they even closed all the saloons! There were 46 of them. These were desperate times! The old biddies from the W. C. T. U. (Women's Christian Temperance Union) might have been smiling from ear to ear but a lot of thirsty tight-jawed men with lowered eyebrows weren't. It was all that damned Dowie's doing.

Attorney Seward, adviser to Mayor Brown, and Attorney Douglass, representing the Dowies, met the train early Sunday morning at Galion and advised the Zion group of the situation

Fig. 41. The entire Mansfield Fire Department was on standby at the City Building ready for action. (Sherman Room collection, M/RCPL.)

recommending they stay away from Mansfield. The Overseer Piper, Elders MClurkin, McFarlane and Evangelist Fisher refused the advice, remained determined to land anyway.

A crowd began to assemble at the Union Station long before east bound Erie train No. 12 was due at 6:35. Warning that rioters would be arrested, the 24 police, Sheriff Pulver with deputies and firemen from the central station were on hand to keep the crowd in check. As the train was seen coming in the crowd surged forward but were restrained by police who kept the depot platform clear. Officers were on the train before it stopped and locked the Pullman doors refusing to let Piper and the elders leave the car. An argument ensued but to no avail. Mayor Brown made an appeal to the crowd to let the law handle

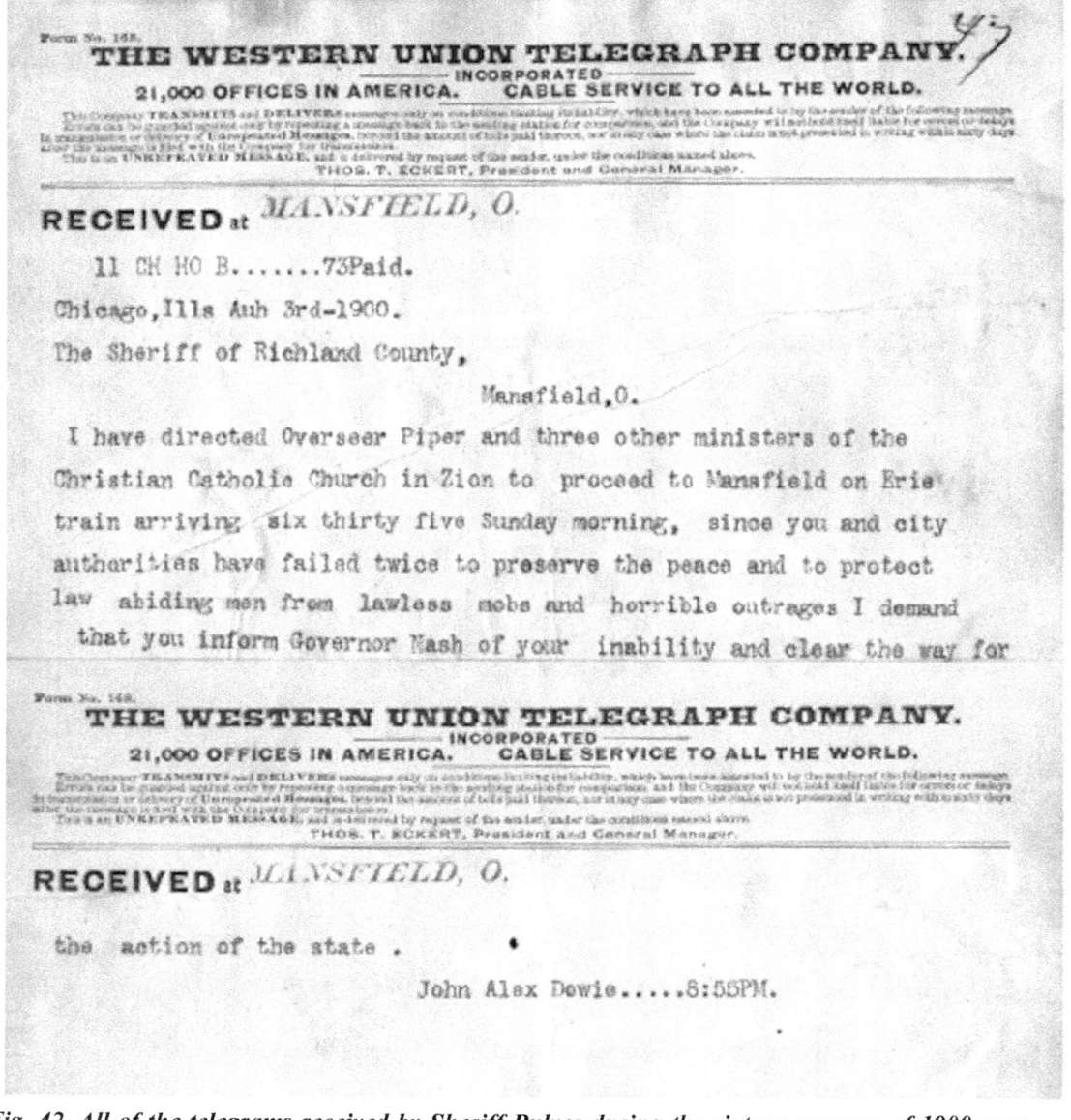

Fig. 42. All of the telegrams received by Sheriff Pulver during the riotous summer of 1900 were collected into a small scrapbook by his daughter Mary Pulver Carter. (Pulver Scrapbook, Robert Carter collection)

the matter. As the train started to pull out the crowd, estimated at over 2,000 standing as far back as Diamond Street, hooted, jeered, and then satisfied, began to leave.

The two lawyers and three policemen stayed on the train and rode as far as Ashland where all got off.

Ashland Times August 8, 1900

Ashland instead of Mansfield entertained the Dowie divine healers Sunday, although a large reception committee was awaiting them in the Richland County metropolis. The why the Zion elders being here was not that they have a church here, but because they were not allowed to get off the train at Mansfield Sunday morning . . . . . As it became known over town that the preachers were here, people gathered to see them though at no time was there a large crowd. The elders from the first declared their intention to return to Mansfield as soon as possible, though they made little effort to return on train 5 at nine o'clock.

When Mansfield officers learned of this move they and many here advised the liverymen that it would mean danger to them and their rigs to drive the Zionites to Mansfield. At the same time officers here wanted the men to get out of the town for fear of trouble, though they advised against their returning to Mansfield.

Piper finally prevailed on H. M. Benner to take them over and paid him $10 and Benner had his horses harnessed when a few gathered in the barn threatened to tear his wagon to pieces and one of his men refused to work for him any longer. Several in the crowd showed the unruly mob spirit in them, but the prompt action of the chief of police Ewing assisted by policeman Buntain, effectively squelched them. One man said in an ordinary tone, "Grab the hose and lets duck him," referring to Piper, and others assented, but Ewing being right there headed off the action that undoubtedly could have led to a disgraceful riot. He also advised the elder to leave the barn after Benner returned the money.

They left the stables amid "hisses and calls" such as "where's the paint" and went back to the hotel and met with Ashland's Mayor Heltman and Sheriff Jones who advised them to go east and avoid Mansfield. They left declaring their intention to return to Mansfield.

When the time came to take train 13 due at 1:47, Rev. Piper and his brethren went to the depot on Hettinger's cab and

Fig. 43. Neither the elbow-benders nor the bartenders in the city's numerous saloons were very happy with the sad state of affairs caused by Dowie's determination to send more ministers to town. The mayor ordered all saloons closed. (Richland County Historical Society)

Fig. 44. AA crowd similar to this was at the station waiting to get their hands on the arriving Dowie elders, but the police prevented them from getting off the train. (Sherman Room collection, M/RCPL)

were met by a crowd of about 500 people. As they went into the depot to purchase tickets for Mansfield they were crowded about by curious people and "where's the paint, tar and feathers" and a few similar remarks were made by the boys but there was no demonstration.

Until the train arrived they were the cynosure of many eyes. Elder Fisher remarked, "You don't often have such a large congregation here Sunday afternoons do you?" They

Fig. 45. Ashland got some unwelcome visitors from Mansfield and a really upset Mayor Heltman gave Mansfield's mayor an earfull. (Sherman Room collection, M/RCPL)

boarded the express train followed by deputy sheriff Grubaugh.

Mayor Heltman was much opposed to the action of the Mansfield officers coming here as they did, and he expressed himself very vehemently in the matter. He gave the deputy sheriff a calling down, and over the phone talked very pointedly to Mayor Brown of Mansfield. He told Brown he considered it an insult for Mansfield police to come here and help excite our people and spread mob contagion, running the risk of attracting the rabble of Mansfield to Ashland. He reminded Brown that his people had always been in the habit of calling Ashland the fifth ward of Mansfield. It was charged that the deputy sheriff indirectly tried to start trouble in Benner's barn to prevent their liveryman giving the elders a rig, and thus keeping them away from Mansfield. Mayor Heltman even went to the extent of drawing up warrants for the arrest of the visiting officers.

The Dowies bought tickets for the 2:20 west bound but their arrival back in Mansfield hit a snag. Before the train stopped Sheriff Pulver with police were in the car and although Piper, with bag in hand, was trying to leave, he was blocked at both ends of the car. Sheriff Pulver was a good sized man who ate well and if he blocked the aisle, the aisle was blocked! "Won't we ever be allowed to come back," asked Piper? "I don't know how long I'll be sheriff but you won't be back while I'm in office," replied Pulver. Police also kept the crowd which had gathered from coming on board. Piper strongly protested, wanted to speak to the crowd but finally agreed to go on to Chicago. There were those in the crowd that feared he would get off at Ontario or Galion and try to sneak back. They would be watching. Many eyes were watching every road, every stranger and every train arrival.

Fig. 46. Richland County Sheriff A. B. Barney Pulver was a good-sized man whose bulk could certainly block a passenger car aisle. He is shown with his prize team of horses. (Robert Carter collection)

Chapter 4
Meanwhile, Back at the Ranch

In the old western "B" movies there was a statement to let everyone know that while the cowboys were fighting off the rustlers in a gun battle, something was going on back at the ranch. In this sequence a look at John Alexander Dowie back in Chicago might be in order.

When Dowie landed in California from Australia he began a career as a roving evangelist between there and Chicago. He tried Evanston, Illinois, Milwaukee, Wisconsin and Minneapolis where little was gained. In 1893 with a few followers he set up a crude tabernacle outside the entrance to the Chicago World's Fair, next to Buffalo Bill Cody's Wild West show and other circus attractions. Dowie began to entice gullible patrons to come inside and fall under the faith healing theory which he had developed. He wrote years later that

Fig. 47. John Alexander Dowie's first tabernacle in America was just outside the entrance to the 1893 Chicago World's Fair. Gunshots from Buffalo Bill's Wild West Show next door punctuated his preaching. (Zion Historical Society)

he was much annoyed when gun shots and war hoops next door spoiled his preaching. He began to draw regular crowds of the curious willing to pay, and from living as a pauper he now developed a financial vision for the future.

From that humble beginning in 1893 he began to gather followers at a rapid rate in Chicago. By 1900 with his faith healing ministry, he prospered to the point that he was reportedly worth $5,000,000 (a huge fortune in those days). As self-appointed General Overseer of the Christian Catholic Church in Zion he claimed a membership of 50,000. He directed a large hospital in a building that paid $25,000 a year rent but employed no physician. He was head of the Zion Bank with $50,000 in capitol where church members were encouraged to deposit funds at 7% interest even though there was never a public financial disclosure of assets. The Illinois State Legislature once made an attempt to get one with no results.

Fig. 48. Dowie's use of the word catholic in the name of his church was evidently meant in the literal definition of 'all embracing,' because he certainly had no kind words for the Roman Catholic Church. The scripture in his logo is from Ezekiel 37:9, a prophecy about raising the dead. If Dowie had managed that we probably would have heard about it. (Huntington Brown scrapbook, Sherman Room collection, M/RCPL)

Fig. 49. Dowie would sometimes brag about his wealth and possessions while preaching and surprisingly his congregation would stand and cheer! His Zion headquarters in the former 300 room Majestic hotel in Chicago was just one of his expensive investments. (Zion Scrapbook collection, Newberry Library, Chicago)

In August of 1900 he bought the older but elegant 300 room Majestic Hotel in downtown Chicago which prompted one newspaper to joke that the rooms had 300 different prices. It was for visiting Zion members and those in need. Dowie and his family lived there most of the time, and all Zion business offices were located there. The cost was $50,000 plus a yearly lot rental of $10,000, payable only in gold, for 99 years. Dowie also owned eight houses in Chicago, several of which might have been "healing" houses. His main nesting place was either the Majestic Hotel or a grand lakeside home nestled in an exclusive neighborhood of wealthy business and industrial tycoons, where he was viewed as the fly in the soup bowl. That getaway place, named Ben MacDhul near Montague, Michigan, was an elaborate

$40,000 "cottage" with a reported $50,000 in furnishings. Situated along the shore of White Lake, north of Muskegon, and surrounded by 200 acres of landscaped grounds it was like a country estate. A local paper once noted that he arrived with servants and three maids. He would want for nothing. He traveled about in a beautiful horse-drawn coach befitting a millionaire.

His greatest scheme was to build "Zion City" on 6,500 acres of land he bought north of Chicago near Waukegan, along Lake Michigan. There was to be a grand tabernacle in the center with main streets leading to it. Church members were encouraged to invest or buy lots and build there and on February 22, 1900 two special twenty-car train loads of prospects estimated at 1,000 persons (which included 200 children and a 150 member choir) went to view the land from a four story tower that had been erected. Dowie rode in his private railroad car away from the common masses. The visitors left the cars to wade to the tower, a mile away, through eight-inch deep snow and slush while elderly and disabled were given sleigh rides. Dowie and family rode in a closed carriage.

The occasion was the fourth anniversary of the founding if the Christian Catholic Church with 5,000 expected to attend. An exhibition of lace and other things to be manufactured at Zion

Fig. 50. On special occasions, when his tabernacle wasn't large enough, Dowie rented the huge Chicago Auditorium. A master preacher and showman, he could attract sizeable crowds. (Chicago Historical Society)

City were displayed. It all sounded good. A few of the faithful bought into the plan and would later begin to build. Others were simply attracted by cheap fares and an outing by train.

It was a disappointing turn out.

A few days later during the celebration at the tabernacle, Dowie made this startling declaration:

The Democrat, Grand Rapids, Feb. 26, 1900

"If I disappear it will be because I shall have been murdered. And I charge that in that event that the Masonic societies and the Methodist Episcopal Church are my murderers. The Masons have taken a vow that they will murder me. The Masons and the Methodist Episcopal Church are today the most murderous institutions on earth. And if I disappear suddenly, it will be because I have been murdered. My death has been sworn."

He accused his followers of being too lazy in their work. "Drones" he called some of them, and he expressed his hatred of drones in vigorous language. "I do not want you," he shouted. "I wish you to the devil. I have not prayed that you go there, but I think I shall."

Charles Miller, a staff reporter for the *Cleveland Plain Dealer*, wrote a lengthy front page feature story on Dowie after careful research. This appeared on September 23 because of interest in the Mansfield violence and riots that were gaining national attention. Portions of his well-written piece are as follows:

. . . . The service which I attended was the afternoon meeting which Mr. Dowie ministers. It was held in the large Michigan Avenue tabernacle building which can seat 2,000 people, perhaps more and was nearly two-thirds full. The audience was made up partly of Mr. Dowie's immediate adherents and more largely of Chicago's miscellaneous population, including many from the army of transients which is constantly moving through the city, and which is easily led to see the eccentric and queer and notorious. In these days of cheap paper and printing it has not been difficult for Mr. Dowie to make himself notorious. The street curbs are sewn thickly with his leaflets, every one of them invariably bearing a portrait of himself in broad expanse of shirt front and full dress. These notices are scattered throughout hotel lobbies and every place strangers are apt to congregate.

The curiosity of Chicago's populace has long been exhausted and Chicago no longer goes to hear him in great numbers, but in a city which is the terminal of 42 lines of railway it is not difficult to draw from its floating population a sufficient number to give him a large audience each Sabbath. His services are given a certain degree of impressiveness, by a large choir frocked in white but is allowed a comparatively small amount of singing. Dowie appeared in a black robe of interminable folds, falling from head to feet, serving to cover his defects of person, most apparent in the form of small bandy legs and large stomach. Though he is large and round he is not tall being less than 5 feet 7 inches.

His head is large, but his eyes are small, and give evidence of cunning rather than frankness or intelligence. His hair is long and bushy on his face but utterly deficient on his head. His feet seem rather large and his hands extremely small in comparison showing that he has been a strange to physical toil. To look at his deep chest and vigorous shoulders one would think that from that deep cavern would come tones of thunder and command. His tones have neither the rich character nor the pleasing tenor of the upper register. They come from the throat and are impeded in their expression not exactly with a lisp, but as though they were handicapped by false teeth to which the owner had not yet become fully accustom. His annunciation is far from perfect and it is necessary for him to give an unpleasant emphasis to everything he says in order to carry his speech to the farthest part of the auditorium. As a speaker it is no secret that Mr. Dowie is a ponderous failure.

Wild Violence is Expected.

. . . . A deplorable ending is expected by most Mansfield citizens. Robert B. McCrory, three times mayor, declared to me openly that the next elder to come to town will be hanged. McCrory is noted to be guarded in his statements, yet what he said was also said by many others with about as little reserve.

DR. DOWIE FAITH HEALER

Says He Has Discovered a Vile Plot.

MASONS AND METHODISTS

He Says, Are Banded Togeth er to Murder Him.

Fig. 52. (Zion scrapbooks, Newberry Library, Chicago.)

Price, One Cent.

DIVINE HEALING SERIES.

DO YOU KNOW GOD'S WAY OF HEALING?

BY

REV. JOHN ALEX. DOWIE.

General Overseer of the Christian Catholic Church.

CHICAGO
ZION PUBLISHING HOUSE
1207 Michigan Ave.
1898

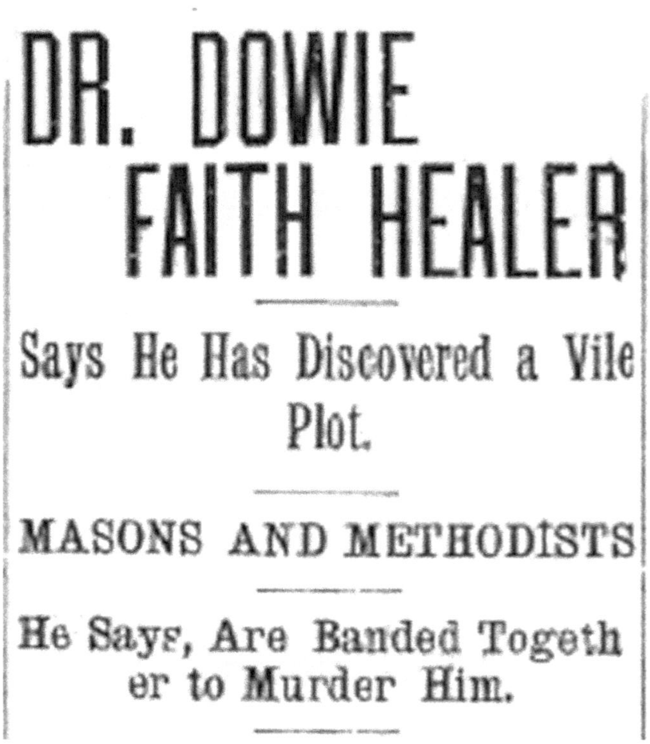

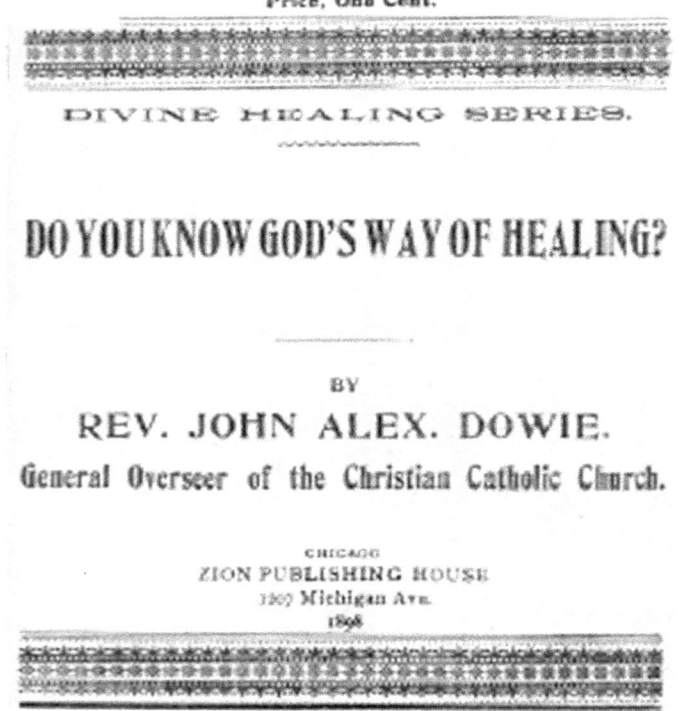

Fig. 51. This religious tract distributed by Zion enthusiasts cost one cent. (Huntington Brown scrapbook, Sherman Room collection, M/RCPL)

Dowie somehow managed to gain a following with his ability to convince people of his healing powers through prayer. Often cited were cures performed on those afflicted with serious ailments, disease, injuries from accidents or alcoholism. A backdrop or altar wall would commonly be decorated with canes, crutches, vials of medicine, cigars, and pipes, bags of tobacco, trusses, and whisky flasks. All were either pointed to as demonstrations of a cure through prayer or instruments of the devil. Spiritual passages as "Abide with Me," "God Is Love," "Jesus Only," "Be Strong in the Lord and the Power of His Works," were placed on the walls. People came from all over the country seeking some kind of a cure. If successful, the Christian Catholic Church could expect a new member. A cash donation was expected but not required.

The word given was see no physician or druggist. They are evil agents of the devil. Alcohol was forbidden and tobacco was deemed an evil substance, as was eating pork or anything with lard in it. His views and preaching often got him into trouble with local authorities and often hecklers or an angry mob would break up his services. The medical community, and in particular medical students, assailed him with missiles of overripe fruit, chemically treated eggs or whatever they could throw. He was threatened and damned by the press and civil authorities. The clergy pounded their pulpits and preached against his teachings.

CENTRAL ZION TABERNACLE,
1621-1633 Michigan Avenue, Chicago, Illinois.

Fig. 53. Dowie bought a large church in Chicago, gutted it, added more balconies, and turned it into his Zion Tabernacle. (Huntington Brown scrapbook, Sherman Room collection, M/RCPL)

Fig. 54. Dowie himself can be seen on stage at the front of his tabernacle in Chicago. (Zion Historical Society)

Dowie's pronounced dislike of all other denominations, be they Protestant, Catholic, Jewish or whatever, was well know but he had a particular dislike for the Methodist Church. The author could find no real explanation for this during research although one report stated the many of Dowie's converts came from Methodist and Catholic churches. The Masons were the chief target of his hatred over all other so called "secret societies" including the Odd Fellows, the Catholic Knights, The Knights of Pythias, The Knights of Labor, The G.A.R. and others. The Masonic Lodges, which had a good number of Methodists, were more numerous and influential. There were five in Mansfield in the late 1890s and among their membership were often found political and business leaders, the movers and shakers of Richland County.

There were other less well-known groups locally. The Knights of Honor, Royal Arcanum, National Union and American Legion of Honor were also a part of the long list of institutions denounced by Dowie. These were male only with some meeting twice a month. One gets the impression for many it was an excuse to have a night or two out from the "ole lady," have a couple of drinks and a good Mansfield cigar. Dowie claimed these groups took men and money away from the work of the church. He hated them.

Fig. 55. A typical Dowie altar arrayed with souvenirs donated by those whom he healed. A caption read: "Some of the crutches, braces, boots, plaster casts, etc. worn by the sufferers that God delivered, with a set of safe blowers tools and the revolver of a burglar, (now reformed) and a number of cots on which divine persons (now healed) were brought to Zion Tabernacle." (Zion scrapbook, Newberry Library, Chicago)

Women were relegated to *Ladies Aid Society's* in five different Mansfield churches and two more had a Women's Missionary Society. There is no record of beer or cigar smoking. These were very proper church ladies, and conducted themselves as such. But they too could join the Ladies of the Maccabees, Ruth Chapter of Eastern Star, Rathbone Sisters, or the Rebecca Lodge of the D. of P.I.O.R.M. Richland Queen Council #55, Degree of Pocohantas, whatever that was. Several other groups accepted both men and women. A lodge meeting was a night out.

Dowie's grand plan for building Zion City would not be complete without the means to make a living once his followers moved there. He announced that a large shoe factory would be built, and incorporated a large manufacturing plant to make lace. During that era lace curtains, coverlets and clothing were in vogue and much of it was imported. During the height of the riots in Mansfield, Dowie made plans for a trip to England for the purpose of buying a lace factory and moving machinery and skilled personnel to Chicago. His aides begged him to postpone the trip.

> "There is no need abandoning your trip," replied the attorney. With this opinion that the legal business of the church was in good condition "Dr." Dowie turned on his "elders" and reprimanded them for their protest. "You act like a bunch of cowards," said "Dr." Dowie. "Suppose I should die, what would become of Zion then? Would you all lay down your arms? I am not only going away, but I now give orders that the elders driven out of Mansfield shall return."

> He said that within two weeks a band of Zionites would "march to Mansfield, despite the dogs there."

Fig. 56. Dowie's Leaves of Healing Zion newsletter condemned the Masons, all "secret societies," and religious denominations of every faith. His publication was like no other and skilled artists were employed to produce eyecatching illustrations. (Huntington Brown scrapbook, Sherman Room collection, M/RCPL)

Fig. 57. Pictured is Mansfield's grandest Masonic Temple on North Main Street at the alley now called Temple Court. Mayor Brown was a member. The Post Office was on the first floor. Mansfield had a host of what Dowie called "secret societies." (Sherman Room collection, M/RCPL)

Fig. 58. Huntington Borwn, Thirty-Third Degree Mason. Past Grand Commander Knights Templar of Ohio.

He said that within two weeks a band of Zionites would "march to Mansfield, despite the dogs there."

The "General Overseer" will leave for Europe tomorrow morning over the Michigan Central railroad and will be accompanied by a party of twelve members of the congregation. Tonight he will hold a reception in the home.

Fig. 59. The Dowie family posed for a portrait in 1899. Dowie and his wife Jane seated, daughter Esther and son Gladstone standing. (Zion Historical Society)

How glad they are to get rid of Dowie in Chicago—even for a few months—may be guessed from the fact that the Michigan Central Railroad gave him a special car for his party and transported his 27 trunks and 24 hand bags free of charge. The Chicago Council would probably extend a vote of thanks to it for removing, even temporarily, a man whom the Council has been trying in vain for six years to drive out of the city.

And then there was this:

The *Columbus Citizen*, Columbus, Ohio. Dowie, accompanied by his wife, son Gladstone, daughter Ester, Elder and Mrs. Stevenson, his bodyguard, the official stenographers and others left Chicago in a private car for New York today enroute to Paris. The luxurious hotel known as Zion where the Dowiets live is two blocks from the depot. Dowie and his wife rode to the station in a coach drawn by four horses

Fig. 60. Dowie mounted his private Michigan Central railroad car bound for New York where he spoke a few words and bid his followers farewell saying, "I shall be gone six months unless the devil gets into Zion." (Chicago Historical Society)

and driven by a coachman in green livery. As Dowie emerged from Zion, a crowd of 1,000 formed lines on the sidewalk. A guard of six Zion policemen surrounded Dowie as soon as he arrived at the Depot. The crowd ran down the street and met the company at the depot subway. Dowie paused at the top of a set of marble stairs and led in song. On arriving at his sumptuously furnished car Dowie mounted the step and spoke, "Twelve years ago there were but two of my children. Now there are 50,000 and hundreds of thousands are rolling in. "Be faithful until death."

Dowie wore a Prince Albert coat of pearl gray material with matching pants, a high rolling collar, a white lawn tie and displayed a diamond of liberal portions on his white shirt front. "I'm going to ride into Jerusalem on a meek and humble ass" continued Dowie. "I shall be gone six months unless the devil gets into Zion."

His remarks were about a dumb as they get. The devil may well have been waiting in Mansfield mobs. As for entering Jerusalem on an ass:

The Times, Louisville, Kentucky, Aug 10 Elder Dowie, the Chicago faith curist and religious faker, impiously announces that he will ride into Jerusalem on an ass. Has he made any arrangements to the manner of exit?

***News Democrat*, Canton, Ohio, Sept. 1.** C. E. McBride suggested that when Dr. Dowie rides into Jerusalem on an ass there will be more than one ass going in.

The Register, Blue Earth, Minnesota, Sept. 9. The Chicago papers say that the notorious Dowie had gone abroad and will ride into Jerusalem on an ass in imitation of the Lord Jesus Christ when on earth. Dowie ought to let the ass ride. It would be more appropriate.

A previous trip to Philadelphia in May had been a disaster. He was heckled, hissed and threatened and required police protection. His collection box was light when he left abruptly. Dowie and his party arrived in New York with little fanfare, stayed in a most expensive Murray Hill Hotel and left the next morning on the Hamburg-American steam ship Graf Walderace bound for Great Britain, northern Africa and Palestine. A good sized crowd of his New York followers bid him farewell at the dock. His group took the best staterooms at a cost of $1,500. To put that into perspective, $1,500 would buy a nice two story house in Mansfield.

And so with a reported $70,000 cash on board (credit cards hadn't been invented yet) Dowie led his group across the sea to gather new converts, buy a lace factory and visit the holy lands. He also sailed away from a nasty situation in a place called Mansfield. That was to be a burr under his saddle that would not soon go away.

Fig. 61. Dowie had a distinctive enough appearance that he was not a difficult subject to caricature, as cartoonists at the Mansfield News discovered in the summer of 1900. (Sherman Room microfilm, M/RCPL)

Chapter 5
Just Tell Them You Saw Me

The Mansfield riots had now been the focus of national attention and the special grand jury convened in an effort to bring law and order out of the whole Dowie mess. Judge Wolfe gave the following charge to the jury on August 5, 1900:

> **Gentlemen of the jury: It is a serious condition of affairs which has its affect on our entire community that has made it advisable to call this special jury. The supremacy of the mob supplanted law. In this city and county these have been a condition of affairs against law and order. For the first time probably in the history of the county we have a jury made up of people outside of the city of Mansfield. We have avoided taking people within the confines of this city, who might be intimidated....And therefore it required the court to look abroad and get men of resolution, courage, taxpayers interested in this controversy, that would say with a strong hand that you the mob shall not prevail. This is not Mansfield alone. I am**

Fig. 62. The Richland County law library received a good deal of use as attorneys A. A. Douglas, county prosecutor Bowers, Judge Wolfe and legal advisors to the mayor all wrestled with legal entanglements involving the Dowies. The library table looks to be filled with off-the-shelf law books. (Sherman Room collection, M/RCPL)

ashamed to say that yesterday when I drove along the streets in the performance of a serious duty, it looked as if our condition was dark, as if the mob had possession. To find people from other towns of our county on the Sabbath day, without a single bit of business, but curiosity, unlawful curiosity, coming here to Mansfield and standing around grinning, to see what was going on.

....We have here in Mansfield, fair ladies, prominent in social circles, high in society, foremost in their position, who say that this man Fockler of the CCC church of Zion, has been saying that the working girls in Mansfield are prostitutes. That has been heralded abroad in this city. Some of the best people in Mansfield say that he has said these things. I want this grand jury to fearlessly investigate that .... I invite all persons who have evidence to come before this grand jury, who have evidence, not mere rumor, but who hear or saw and can testify that they heard Fockler say these things.

And with that, witnesses were called and the process began. Oddly enough the carefully picked out-of-town jurors had a fine line to hold. During the riots many of those involved were farmers and Sheriff Pulver remarked that farmers and delegations from Plymouth, Shelby and Shiloh were coming to Mansfield on the weekends to watch the fun. The Lexington and Bellville bunch would also be on hand. It was free entertainment. By August 11, some 78 people had been examined, 25 cases considered and 17 indictments issued. Sheriff Pulver went to Canton with a warrant for elder Fockler. He was unable to find him.

Fig. 63. Company M of the Ohio National Guard was a rugged group of dedicated men. Not all of them could be trusted, however, when it came to calming a riot, especially Sergeant William "Red" Hartman. (Sherman Room collection, M/RCPL)

Fig. 64. The August 11, 1900 issue of <u>Leaves of Healing</u> didn't make many friends in Mansfield. Goddess Zion warned the Masons, Governor Nash and Mayor Brown that the wrath of God would fall upon them. (Huntington Brown scrapbook, Sherman Room collection, M/RCPL)

One of those arrested was William "Reddy" or "Red" Hartman who was evidently one of the mob ring leaders or possibly the main one. He was identified as such by Overseer Piper and mentioned in the news. Hartman was arrested by Deputy Tom Bell as he walked past the jail. He had just returned from New Philadelphia where he had been at camp with Company M of the Eighth Regiment of the Ohio National Guard. Like the others, he posted a $300 bond and was released.

On August 10th another issue of Leaves of Healing hit the streets which did nothing to ease the tense feelings that gripped the area. Depicted was the Goddess Zion pointing her Word of God sword at the evil Masonic mob monster holding a tar bucket and paint can while Governor Nash and Mayor Brown trample on the Constitution which granted free speech and worship.

The Dowie elders were persistent in their effort to preach in Mansfield. On Sunday, August 12 two new Elders, W. O. Dinius and Silas Moot, quietly arrived in town by the back door. The depots were still being watched by police and small crowds so the two passed through on the Pennsylvania and got off at Lucas on Saturday evening. The next

Fig. 65. The former home of E. H. Leiby is still standing at the corner of East Second and Foster Streets. In the ensuing decades after the events of 1900 the building served as a boarding house/hotel and then a restaurant before its restoration began in 2008.

morning they hired a buggy to take them back to Mansfield where they registered at the Vonhof Hotel. After being served breakfast they unfortunately let it be known who they were and the management ordered them out of the hotel. They intended to go to the E. H. Leiby residence at the corner of East Second and Foster streets to preach. Being new in town they were not immediately recognized but word of their intentions spread like wildfire and by the time Mayor Brown, attorney Seward and four police officers arrived at the house a crowd of nearly 200 was on hand.

Inside the house singing could be heard indicating services were beginning. Brown and Seward went in while police watched the crowd, but in the ensuing discussion where the imminent danger was pointed out, the two preachers remained adamant in their intentions to stay. They had written instructions from Dowie himself to preach and remain in Mansfield "at all hazards." After considerable persuasion from lawyer Seward, and noticing the gathering crowd outside, the two Dowies reluctantly agreed to leave for the peace of city. A two-seat carriage was waiting outside and two officers drove the Elders to Crestline. There was no violence but the crowd reportedly "hooted" as they left. It was evidently a very long, slow buggy ride intended to prevent their charges from returning to Mansfield by train in time for an afternoon service. The preachers bitterly complained but to no avail.

Elders Dinius and Moot checked into the Emerson House in Crestline Sunday evening and early the next morning hired a young man to drive them back to Mansfield. With the stations still being watched they arrived with little notice at the downtown square about 9 AM and went immediately to the office of attorney A. A. Douglass. Soon Mayor Brown and several police officers arrived, as did a curious crowd gathering outside. While a meeting was going on inside something else was happening in the park as reported in the *Mansfield Shield and Banner*.

> **A young man by the name of David Strauch, who resides on a farm south of Crestline, drove the Zionites to the city from Crestline in a rig belonging to his father. He hitched his horse on North Walnut Street and sauntered down to Central Park and sat down on a bench. He boasted that he had driven the Zion elders to Mansfield and that he was not afraid. His remarks were overheard and**

a hurried conference was held among the men who had congregated. A couple of men got into an argument with the young farmer near the fountain. Suddenly he was thrown backwards head first into the fountain with a splash. One of the crowd went in with him but was hurriedly helped out and ran away. The water was deep and when the young farmer came to the surface he choked, gasped and sputtered. He was helped out and presented a ludicrous, pitiable sight. Thoroughly frightened, with water dripping from him at every step, was taken to police headquarters where he was put in bed in the women's quarters and his clothes were hung up to dry.

Fig. 66. The splash of David Staunch was duly immortalized by the Mansfield News *cartoonist for the front page of August 14, 1900. (Sherman Room microfilm, M/RCPL)*

At the meeting in the lawyer's office it was decided that the two elders were to be driven out of the city. A dinner was ordered from the Vonhof and served on a table in the law office. A carriage was ordered and police officers Austin and Madden loaded them up along with young man dunked in the fountain and started for Crestline. As they left a large crowd "cheered lustily." Though it was not recorded, the elders must have been bitching and complaining all the way about their treatment, which caused the police escort to dump all three out a mile or so west of Ontario. They could walk the rest of the way.

A new fad was reported in the *Mansfield News*. The latest craze was a little ultramarine blue button with a picture of crossed paint brushes in the center which would identify the wearer as a member of the mob that painted the Dowie. It had become rather popular.

Worried Of Their Fruitless Struggle Are The Zionites
It Is Thought The Trouble Is Over

That was the headline on Tuesday the 14th of August. There were several factors which prompted this optimism. First, on the carriage ride towards Crestline the elders said that they didn't think they would be allowed to remain in Mansfield. They could not leave their assignment until they were given permission from Overseer Piper, however, and so they would telegraph the situation to him. They wanted permission to go home.

Fig. 67. The "Mansfield Blues" button worn by many Mansfield residents involved in painting the Dowie preachers was a symbol of great pride and a warning to future Elders. (Sherman Room microfilm, M/RCPL)

Second, was a meeting between Mayor Brown, attorney Seward and Mr. and Mrs. Leiby, the recognized head of the Mansfield Zion church. They agreed to hold no more services during the week, and only quietly among the members on Sunday. No Zion preachers were to be present.

Attorney A. A. Douglass received a telegram from Overseer Piper requesting him to come to Chicago for a meeting. This was seen as a signal that the Zion church "had wearied of their unsuccessful attempts to in invade Mansfield, and is willing to arbitrate." Douglass and his law partner attorney L. C. Mengert had been retained months earlier to represent elder Fockler and the Mansfield Zion church.They left later that evening, picked up elders Moot and Dinius at Crestline and on their way to Chicago. The two elders had received permission from Piper to go home.

The grand jury finished its work on Wednesday and, although Judge Wolfe was somewhat disappointed in their work, he thanked them for their service and they all were treated to a round of good Mansfield made cigars.

Mayor Brown, Sheriff Pulver and other elected officials were in a relaxed and what was described as a "jovial" mood. Many folks in and around Mansfield, including the darned farmers, thought that they had won out over Alexander Dowie and his Christian Catholic Church in Zion. No more elders, no more mobs, no more violence and arrests. The bad publicity would go away.

HOPES SHATTERED

That evening attorney James Seward, working with the mayor, received a telegram from A. A. Douglass in Chicago:

> **Just concluded conference.   Attitude unchanged and can't be changed. Impossible.**

Then the *Shield and Banner* obtained a copy of a telegram sent to the one of the Elders just after they left Crestline. The newspaper dutifully printed it:

> **Stay in Mansfield even if you have to seal your testimony with your life's blood.If they refuse, they make themselves liable to fines fixed by law in such cases. Say to Mayor Brown that our forbearance with his disgraceful acts have about reached their limits. Ask him how much money he wants to put into Zion's coffers by his illegal acts of driving inoffensive, law abiding citizens from Mansfield. Tell sheriff**

and mayor to fill the cup of their official mobocracry, but Zion, with God's help, will establish the right to preach the everlasting Gospel in Mansfield even if it takes her last dollar and her last man....Zion is praying for you and elder Moot. Keep me posted....Signed, William Hamner Piper

At 6:35 AM Sunday, August 19, two men wearing dark clothing and beards stepped off the Erie Eastbound bound passenger train No. 12. James Barrett, the new chief of police, noticed the men and upon inquiry found they were Evangelist W. E. Moody and Elder S. A. Walton. They were sternly invited by the chief and two officers to a meeting with the mayor at the county jail where they were informed that would not be permitted to preach and were detained. They were served lunch but refused pork as it was against their belief and would eat no pie as the crust had lard in it. They were later taken to the depot and, against their will, put on the westbound Erie train No.13 for Chicago.

The *Mansfield News* carried the headline; "Just Tell Them That You Saw Me." The story filled two columns. There were no large crowds and no violence was evident at their departure. The work of the grand jury and the arrests had put a damper on those inclined to mob actions. It was simply Dowies in, Dowies out.

POLICE CHIEF FIRED

Under a headline which read, "Chief's Position Now Vacant, Climax Reached," the *Mansfield Daily Shield* carried the details in a brief column.

> As a result of misconduct on the part of Chief Clark on several occasions, he is now out of a position on the city police force. The climax came last night when Clark was taken out of the Vonhof bar and put to bed in a hotel by one of the force. He refused to stay and was taken to the city prison by Captain Crider and locked up for drunkenness.

> This morning Clark was relieved of his badge, helmet and revolver by Mayor Brown and discharged. The Public are fully aware of things that have happened in the past which did not reflect highly on the administration brought about by the conduct of Chief Clark.

> "This last affair was the straw that broke the camel's back," said Mayor Brown to a Shield man this morning, "and Sam Clark cannot remain longer in the public service." Mayor

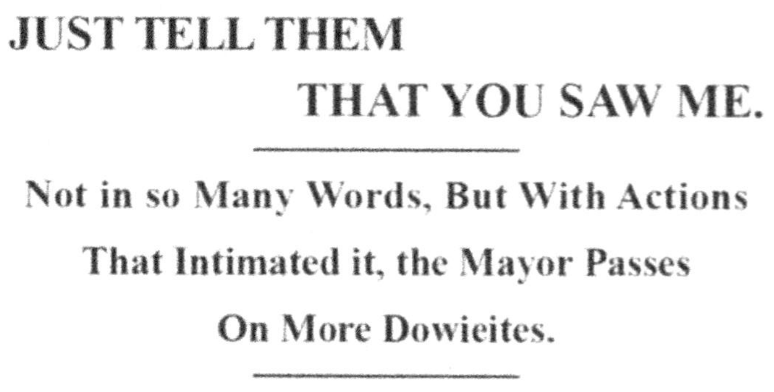

JUST TELL THEM THAT YOU SAW ME.

Not in so Many Words, But With Actions

That Intimated it, the Mayor Passes

On More Dowieites.

Fig. 68. The newspapers were not without a sense of humor during much of the fracas: the Mansfield News *carried this headline on August 20. (Sherman Room microfilm, M/RCPL)*

Brown stated that the affair was most unfortunate but he could put up with Clark's conduct no longer.

Now that Chief Clark had been fired, one would expect his replacement would be a man with previous experience in law enforcement, a man with keen eyes who was tough and capable of righting any wrong that came his way, a man with a strong management and leadership background. That would surely be the choice.

Fig. 69. James Barrett (left) replaced fired Chief of Police Clark (right) who got plastered once too often. One of his own officers had to put him in jail for drunkenness. (Mansfield Police Department archives)

Those qualifications didn't exactly fit the man chosen on August 17. The new Chief, James Barrett, 38, had been a janitor at the Hedges Street School, a position he had held for five years. Before that he had worked at the Altman-Taylor Company where they made steam engines and thrashing machines. Evidently the main reason he got the nod over the other applicants was because Barrett had served as a Republican central committeeman

Fig. 70. The August 18, 1900 Leaves of Healing once again in viscious cartoon style took Mayor Brown and local denominational ministers to task for running Dowie's preachers out of town. Shown are the tar bucket and paint can while the minister spills sugar-coated sermons from a plate of pulpit taffy. (Huntington Brown scrapbook, Sherman Room, M/RCPL)

for the ninth ward. It was simply a political appointment! No physical description or qualificationsof the new chief was offered.

The new janitor turned police chief had his work cut out for him. The next day another *Leaves of Healing* hit the streets showing the Goddess Zion with her Word of God sword ready to defeat Mayor Brown, Satan holding a tar bucket and a denominational minister spilling a plate of "pulpit taffy." If that didn't set people on edge nothing else would.

The following Sunday it was business as usual. Elder Ephriam Bassinger from Bluffton came in on the Erie at the usual time. Either he didn't look like a Dowie elder or else was disguised and succeeded in slipping through the crowd past police. He headed straight for the Leiby house and as he and others began arriving neighbors noticed and called the police. The janitor Police Chief Barrett and one of his officers hustled Bassinger and another minister who had spent the night at Leibys off to sheriff Pulver's jail or "Pulver's Parlor" as the press called the county lock up. The other minister was from the Church of God and was a friend just visiting. He was released but Bassinger got the usual afternoon police march to the Erie depot and sent west. Bassinger had been advised by the sheriff, the mayor and Attorney Seward that it was not safe for him to remain.

Figs. 71 and 72. The <u>Mansfield News</u> was unable to print photographs in 1900, so they relied on their staff cartoonist to provide appropriate illustrations. He evidently had a wry sense of humor that must have brought smiles to readers who were not members of the Dowie congregation. (Sherman Room microfilm, M/RCPL)

He would return a week later on August 19, with the same results. There was growing concern by many over the piling up of damage law suits against the city and county. How long would this go on?

Fig. 73. A <u>Mansfield News cartoon of Chief Barrett</u>

Chapter 6
Divine Healing and Habeas Corpus. Divine Healing?

There were those who firmly believed in John Alexander Dowie and his faith healing methods. Did prayer alone cure the sick of body as well as mind? Did Dowie and his elders have the ability through prayer alone to bring a Divine healing to the needy? Were testimonials to their success legitimate, or prompted by Elders convincing uneducated parishioners that almighty God had brought a Divine healing to the afflicted through prayers? On the other hand, there were wealthy businessmen and prominent public officials who belonged to that denomination as well. It left more than a few scratching their heads.

The *Cleveland World* carried this Mansfield story;

> **Of course, many people here who do not endorse the vituperation indulged there by the Zion elders, nevertheless, privately cling to a belief in Dowie's system of salvation healing. Many persons in town are cited as having been healed. A notable case is that of Street Commissioner Hoffman. For years he was a helpless invalid, being so crippled in his limbs that he could not walk a step. He was a prominent cigar manufacturer, and in his wheel chair was a familiar figure. His was supposed to be a hopeless case. He tried almost all systems of treatment with no success until he went to Dowie in Chicago. He left his chair there and may be seen walking briskly about Mansfield now at almost any hour of the day. Everybody in the town knows of his cure. None attempt to answer the argument it presents.**

Other cures were reported and read by skeptical readers.

> *The Reporter*, Logansport, Indiana
>
> **Mr. and Mrs. M. G. Stewart are selling their residence and other real estate and moving to Dowie's city of Zion. The Stewarts claim to have gained their faith through taking the Dowie treatment. Mrs. Stewart, suffering from a chronic ailment, was cured instantly by Dowie's laying on of hands. She claims her son Luther was cured of hasty consumption by the same treatment last November and that when her husband two years ago was so low with typhoid fever that his life was despaired of she telegraphed Dowie to pray for him, and shortly after the message had been delivered the victim began to improve and within three days sat up at the table and ate his dinner.**

There were other testimonials, both local and from other places. To this day there are those well respected in the medical profession who attest to the power of prayer and its connection to patient's recovery. Both physician and patient seek God's blessing and helping hand.

Divine healing was one thing but could a "Divine" message from the Almighty also come to question?

> **The *Mansfield News* August 14, 1900.**
>
> **Galion: The Reformed Church was struck by lightning Sunday. During the morning services about 11:00 o'clock there was a sharp flash of lightning and a ball of fire dropped through the ceiling of the gallery, floated out of an east window and exploded between the church and the residence of Postmaster Cupp. Aside of a small hole torn in the roof and ceiling no damage was done, although members of the congregation were very nervous. A horse tied in the church yard was knocked down and badly shocked but recovered in a short time.**

Could this be construed as some sort of a Divine message? Was this in response to a really bad sermon? Or was it because the congregation wasn't paying attention? Perhaps it was simply an act of nature but one could draw several conclusions from the story. Though not recorded, one would guess after church more than a few present that morning had to go straight home, change their undergarments and locate the family bible.

AN INJUNCTION

The Zion leaders in Chicago didn't quite get the message from Mansfield. Each week Overseer Piper sent Elders to preach but they were jailed and sent back by train. On August 20, it was reported Elder Bassinger made the usual quick round trip with police and a small crowd following every step. That same week Judge Wolfe issued a temporary injunction returning the use of the tabernacle to the Zion church, however a police officer was stationed there the next week to see that no services were held. Bassinger made three more Sunday jail round trips on August 26, September 2nd and 9th. He was under orders to do so but some taxpayers were feeling uneasy about all the possible damage suits that might be piling up.

This continued until September 16, when the Zion's attorney A. A. Douglass went to the Mayor and informed him that the Elder Ephriam Bassinger was in town and invited the mayor to have him arrested. Douglass had an injunction and a "writ of habeas corpus" in his pocket which in legal terms would prevent the Mayor, the police or the sheriff from interfering with Bassinger's movement in town. The writ had been prepared in Chicago. Mayor Brown decided to let the Dowie Elde r into the city and let him take his chances, as the police had been rendered almost powerless under threat of the injunction.

A writ of habeas corpus can be used in certain extraordinary circumstances where there is unlawful restraint of a person's liberty and there is no adequate remedy in ordinary course of law. Thus, one purpose of habeas corpus is to secure immediate relief from illegal confinement. In this case, Bassinger was now on his own to go where he wished without police interference or jail. The hands of the police were tied and they were ordered not to touch him under penalty of a lawsuit.

Attorney Douglass was really feeling the heat and had to publish in the newspapers an explanation of his re- sponsibilities as the Zion lawyer for which he had been hired. He did not approve of some of their actions but his job was to represent their interests. Douglass had received many threats both verbally and by mail.

Bassinger spent the night at the Balliet's home near Lu- cas, and with several followers went to the E. H. Leiby home on East Second Street on Sunday morning where about 30 more were waiting. All were jubilant over the victory they thought they had achieved over the Mayor, the police and the mobs. Their joyous celebration was short-lived however as outside a curious crowd began to assemble from all directions and no police were to be seen. As reported in the Shield and Banner:

The crowd assembled around the house and after consultation decided to hustle the elder out of the city. The house was struck by stones and missiles thrown by members

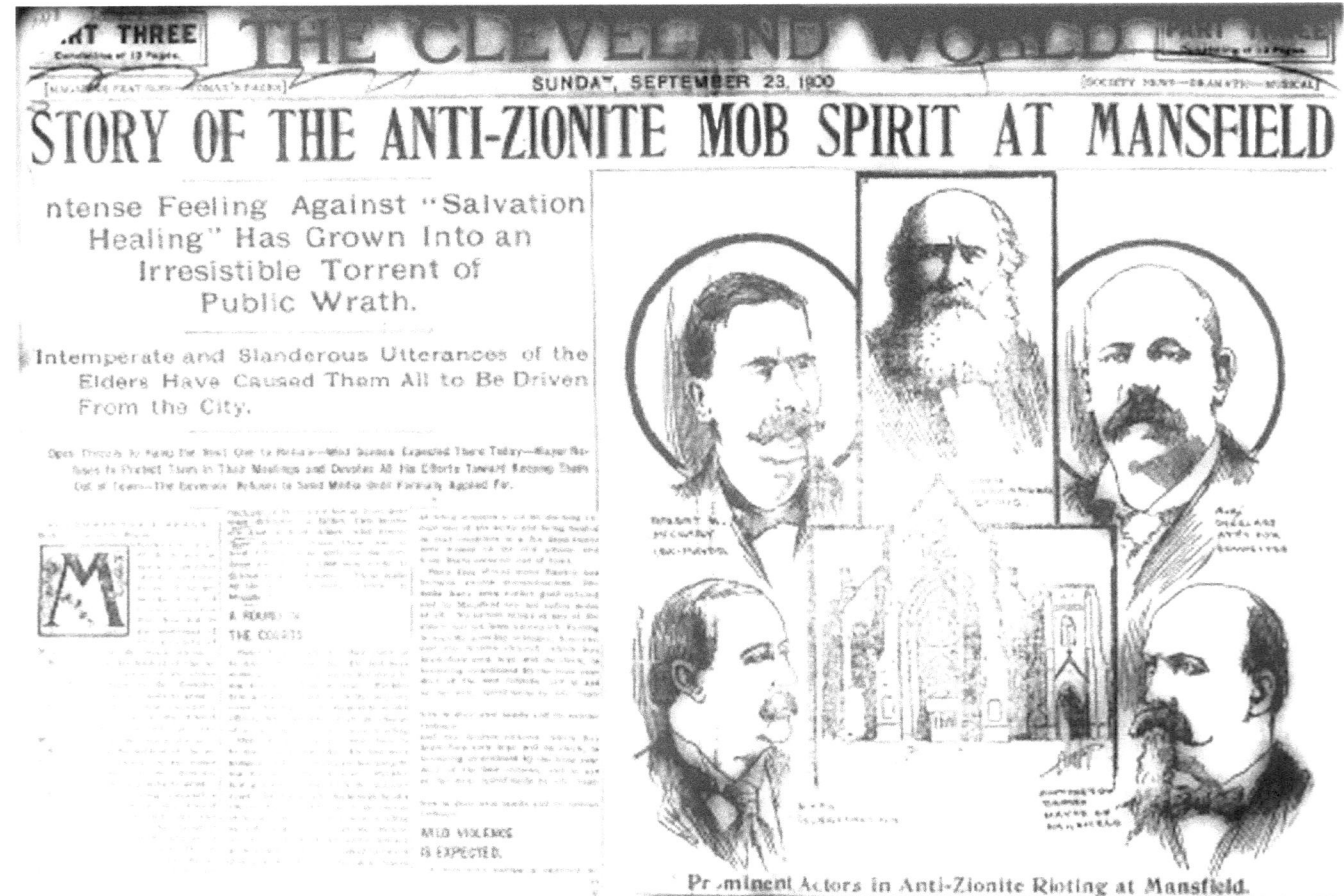

Fig. 74. Mansfield made the front page of the Cleveland World and other newspapers around the country, much to its own chagrin. Interest in the conflict was growing day by day. (Zion scrapbook, Newberry Library, Chicago)

of the mob and windows broken. Attorney J. P. Seward, who was down in the city, heard that the mob assembled at the Leiby home and hurried to the scene. He found the mob meant business and delivered to them a short pointed talk. The mob agreed they would not molest Bassinger if Seward would take him out of the house and down to the depot.

Seward knocked on the door and a couple of women opened the door slightly and refused him entrance but he forced his way past them. Bassinger was concluding services and was informed it would be best for him to leave to which he agreed. A buggy was brought around back for Seward but the mob drove it away in a shower of rocks and dirt. Bassinger would have to endure a long dangerous walk across town to the station.

When Bassinger stepped out of the house the mob broke into wild cheers and surged around the Elder. Bassinger thought his time had come but the mob kept its word and he was not molested. Bassinger was escorted across Foster Street to Park Avenue East and thence to the court house, followed by the jeering, hooting mob which increased at every step. Seward held Bassinger by one arm and two elderly women, Dowie followers, held on to the other and flourished umbrellas. Arriving at the court

Fig. 75. The old Methodist Church on the Square was a landmark and witness to many mob scenes. Built in 1870, it was renovated in 1906 into the present structure. (Robert Carter collection.)

house the women were advised that the best thing they could do was make them self scarce, and they went away.

As the ever-increasing mob escorting Bassinger approached the square that Sunday morning the Methodist Church was just letting out. One has to wonder if Alexander Dowie's earlier words, "I might disappear at any time, the Methodists and Masons are plotting to murder me," might have crossed Bassinger's mind when he looked ahead and his eyes beheld a whole bunch of those damned Methodists pouring out into the square. The other congregations, the Catholics, Lutherans, and so on were also letting out. Perhaps all who had just come from a worship service had to wrestle with a tough decision; look down their nose with disgust at the whole affair, join the mob,—or just go on home and eat Sunday chicken dinner. The second choice must have appealed to many. The mob began to swell. It was a Sunday morning in Mansfield like no other in the State of Ohio. Where else could one come out of a prayer filled worship service of brotherly love, enduring faith, and forgiveness of sin to join a mob intent on beating the hell out of an Elder?

As Bassinger was hurried along, the mob, which numbered 3,000 at least, cheered lustily. As Bassinger was jostled along down North Diamond Street, decayed fruit, dirt and even brickbats, were thrown at the elder from the backwoods. Some of the fruit hit Mr. Seward on the nose and other parts of his anatomy. Chief Barrett, who followed along with the crowd, was struck several times by fruit and stones

Fig. 76. The Dowie Elders and Deacons were unwelcome arrivals at the Union Station, and were hooted and jeered at when they left. (Sherman Room collection, M/RCPL)

intended for the Dowieites. The police followed along but they took no hand in quieting the disturbance.

When the mob arrived about noon at the depot with Bassinger he was only too glad to call on the authorities for protection. He was placed in the Erie waiting room and guarded by Chief Barrett, Deputy Sheriff Bell, officers, Mckay, Madden, Austin and Slaybaugh. The crowd gathered outside and jeered at Bassinger through the windows. Mayor Brown and attorney Seward advised him to leave the city.

Mob Disappears From Depot.

The mob at the depot disappeared soon after Bassinger was taken into the waiting room but subsequent events proved it had other business to transact. Mr. and Mrs. E. H. Leiby, who introduced the Dowie religion in this city, have made themselves obnoxious to the mob and it was determined that Leiby should also leave the city. Accordingly they visited the Leiby home again and demanded Leiby. He locked himself in the dining room and refused to come out. The angry mob broke down the door and made its way into the kitchen. The door separating the kitchen from the dining room was also broken down and Leiby dragged from the house, down Foster to East Fourth Street, up Fourth to Diamond, and thence to the depot.

When Leiby entered the waiting room at the depot, James P. Seward gave him an emphatic calling down as follows; "Leiby, you brought this all on yourself and you are a sneaking liar. What did you do a short time ago but give your solemn promise to Mayor Brown and myself, in this office that you would not allow the Dowie elders to stay in your house let alone hold Sunday services." Leiby feebly protested that there may have been some misunderstanding, but this only made Seward angrier and Leiby was given a talking to that he will not soon forget.

Frank Calver, another Dowie friend of Leiby, had also been dragged along and with Bassinger the trio bought tickets west bound for Crestline. The Elder, who was described as being white as a sheet when he arrived at the station, expressed some fear that if his identity was discovered when he got there he would be in trouble. They were escorted from the Erie station to the Pennsylvania & Ft. Wayne depot, put on the last car of the mail train and amid a jeering, cheering crowd, were off to Crestline.

A crowd of angry women also visited the Leiby home to escort Mrs. Leiby out of town but she must have seen the hand writing on the wall and had gone to the country. A police guard was placed at the house in response to threats to burn it down. The next day Attorney Douglas said he received 25 telephone calls ordering him out of the city!

The injunction and writ of habeas corpus had not achieved the result Overseer Piper had expected.

Fig. 77. There was more than one way to tell a story. Elder Bassinger and friends were excorted to the station by a good-sized crowd that evidently had little else to do. (Sherman Room microfilm, M/RCPL)

Chapter 7
About Petered Out

That was the headline in the September 20, 1900 edition of the *Mansfield News* after word was received by local officials that no Dowie elders would be coming the next Sunday. At least that was the word from Overseer Piper. Added to this was the news that the Leibys' finally had had enough and were going rent their house and move to Chicago. It was also noted that the Zion congregation was shrinking. At one time months earlier there were about 70 at the tabernacle but services at the Leiby house could muster less than 40. By the time of the latest mob attack only a few were in attendance. Some members left through fear, others in disgust over the continual controversy, but those with children in school left due to the cruel harassment their youngsters were receiving. It was an unpleasant experience for a family to belong to the Mansfield congregation. The loss of friends, neighbors and sometimes employment was just too much.

The Reputation Our City Is Getting Abroad

That was the headline in the *Mansfield Daily Shield* which copied the following from an old and highly respected Chicago newspaper. A portion is reprinted here:

> ***Chicago Chronicle*, Sept. 22, 1900**
>
> **The continuance of mob rule in the town of Mansfield, O., has now assumed the proportions of a national scandal. If Authorities of the state are unable or unwilling to protect citizens it is time to call on the federal government under constitutional provision which guarantees the states a republican form of government and which provides that citizens may not be deprived of life, liberty or without due process of law. There is neither government nor law in Mansfield, Ohio. Residents of other states have been mobbed and expelled from the town repeatedly within the past few weeks. Last Sunday several taxpayers and residents of the city itself were taken from their homes by a mob and driven out of town, being menaced by tar and feathers and even death if they returned.**

Attorney Seward had just gone to the Leiby house on his own, not for his position as an agent for the mayor, and was drawn into the riot by chance. He received a good deal of criticism from the public who felt he had acted on the wrong side. The newspapers with few new riot stories picked up smaller items:

> **A. A. Douglass and J. P. Seward had a controversy on Main Street shortly after 6 o'clock Sunday evening. It is understood that Douglass undertook to take Seward to task for the advice he and C. E. McBride had given the mayor. Seward told Douglas that he did not interfere with the advice that he was giving the Dowies and he didn't want any from him. Seward enumerated a few of the offices that Douglass has held as well as his relatives and suggested that he owed it to the people of Mansfield to**

lend a hand in helping to keep order here where his interests are centered. The debate waxed pretty warm and some other things were said which would not look well in print.

In Chicago, Overseer Piper must have been fuming! On September 19th he sent Ohio Governor Nash a 1,288 word telegram (that must have set some kind of a record) in which he outlined in great detail the dates of mob violence and the number of times his people were jailed, sent out of town or prevented from leaving their train car. It was written in a respectful manner and appealed for help from the National Guard.

Fig. 78. Overseer Piper and out-of-town newspaper reporters kept the telegraph operators busy in the summer of 1900. (Sherman Room microfilm, M/RCPL)

...At least two officers of our church will be in Mansfield next Lords Day to conduct services. I am giving you ample opportunity to have sufficient militia there Saturday to preserve law and order on the Lords Day the 23rd. inst....We have scores of officers and thousands of lay members who are willing to die, if necessary, for the cause of Christ. We shall never cease to demand our right to proclaim the Gospel of Jesus Christ to the members of our church in Mansfield. If people do not wish to come and hear, it is their privilege to stay away. I believe it will be necessary in order to put down the awful spirit of lawlessness that has been reigning in Mansfield, for these two months that you keep the militia there for some days especially over the Lord's Day Sept. 30.

Governor Nash chose not to get involved but Mayor Brown went to Columbus to consult with him. There was always the question as to whether the local men in Company M of the Ohio National Guard could be trusted. One member, William "Red" Hartman, was one of the mob ring leaders. The local papers reprinted the full text of the telegram and it had the effect of putting everybody on edge ready for the next round of Dowie Sunday invasions.

A BLACK SUNDAY

Right on cue early Sunday morning September 23rd more trouble rolled in on the Erie from the west. A reporter from the *Mansfield Daily Shield* filed this story:

> Another anti-Dowie demonstration occurred in Mansfield, yesterday. Dowie elders Ephriam Bassinger of Bluffton, and Silas Moot of Lima alighted from Erie train no. 12 at 6:35 o'clock Sunday morning and were immediately recognized by a crowd of about 50 people who were at the depot. The elders endeavored to hire a cab but the cab men refused them. The elders started to walk up North Diamond Street but when in front of Frank's Brewery they were intercepted by a crowd of about 200 people. Moot showed fight and he was pummeled and kicked. He had a badly disfigured right eye and damaged nose. Bassinger was also kicked and roughly handled.
>
> The two were taken down North Diamond Street to the Erie tracks and down the tracks to the Richland Buggy Company's plant where they were ordered to disrobe. Bassinger obeyed willingly but Moot resisted. His clothes were torn from him. The two were then daubed from head to foot with sticky roof tar. Liberal quantities were poured on their hair and in their beards. They were allowed to don their outer clothing and in charge of 250 people they were escorted up the tracks to North Diamond Street followed by an ever increasing mob. The two victims presented a sorry looking sight. Tar glistened in hair and beards. A once white collar daubed with black paint hung around Moot's neck, one trouser leg was rent twain and impeded Moot's progress and exposed tarred flesh. A tattered hat was placed on his head. Bassinger wore a raincoat and battered hat.

Fig. 79. The background of this crowd scene at the Union Station shows the Buggy Works that figured in accounts of mob activity during the riot season. (Sherman Room Collection, M/RCPL.)

Exhibited Through the Streets

The elders were taken up North Diamond to Fifth and up Main. When Central Park was reached it is estimated there were 3,500 people in the mob. Someone yelled, "Take them to Leiby's" and the march was continued down Park Avenue East, past the Zion tabernacle where services were to be held. A long procession of vehicles followed the mob down Park Avenue East. Arriving at the Leiby home it was found that they had left the city. A short stop was made and they were given a talking to by a local saloon keeper. The elders were ordered to pray and shutting his uninjured eye Moot offered a short prayer. The elders promised the mob they would leave the city at once if they were

Fig. 80. The Mansfield Square could fill up quickly with people from all over the county, for a parade, civic event, or a spontaneous riot. (Phil Stoodt collection.)

taken to the depot. At the carriage works Bassinger swore he would never return to Mansfield.

The march resumed and the elders were taken down the tracks to East Fifth Street, arm and arm with the saloon keeper who had taken charge of them. When the mob reached the corner of Fifth and Main a squad of police under charge of Mayor Brown and Chief Barrett alighted from a street car and took the elders in charge. The police and their charges were followed by a shouting, jeering mob to the city prison.

Fig. 81. With the streets teeming with people it is surprising there weren't more injuries from trampling and negligent jaywalking. (Sherman Room collection, M/RCPL)

The two saloon keepers leading the mob were Mike Weil and Bill Sylvester. Weil was a saloon keeper and gambler who ran the "Old Homestead Saloon" at 23 North Foster Street. It featured "Red Band Lager Beer." They paraded the two Dowies from street to street promising that they were taking them to safety until they were intercepted by the police. The following Monday Weil and Sylvester rented a rig and slowly drove around town bowing to the left and right, as heroes of the hour. Mayor Brown made no effort to stop them, and reportedly laughed at the sight.

> *Philadelphia North American,* September 24 Mansfield, Ohio, Another anti-Dowie demonstration occurred here today, when elder Moot of Lima and Bassinger of Bluffton, sent to Mansfield by order of Overseer Piper, of Chicago, received a coat of tar from infuriated citizens. Several Dowie elders have been mobbed and sent out of the city and warned never to return, but these warnings have had no effect.

SMOKESTACK VARNISH

At the jail Sheriff Pulver, prosecutor Bowers, Health Officer Craig, attorney Seward, Coroner Bushnell, (well you never know) two doctors and a reporter were inside. Lard, benzene and Vaseline were secured and, wearing blue coveralls with sleeves rolled up, Seward and Officer Wilson spent more than an hour removing what was called "smokestack varnish" from the elders. One account said it was tar mixed with a drying agent used to seal buggy wheels. It had started to dry and must have been a tough chore to remove. After a bath they were give medical examinations and new clothing. Beaten and bruised, neither was seriously injured. At noon they were taken by police escort to the depot and sent west. A crowd had remained outside the police station but caused no trouble.

Fig. 82. Bassinger and Muth were good fodder for the Mansfield News cartoonists. The local mob made news all across the United States. (Sherman Room microfilm, M/RCPL)

With that many people who skipped church and had nothing else to do on Sunday morning why should they just go home? When the eastbound 10:40 AM came in on the Pennsylvania & Ft. Wayne there were an estimated 2,000 eager people waiting as there had been a rumor that Overseer Piper might be coming. He didn't but unfortunately a gentleman from Crestline by the name of L. A. Fisher did get off the train and when it became known his name was Fisher the crowd mistook him for the elder Fisher who had been painted. He was roughly handled until someone from Crestline identified him. Besides the name, he wore whiskers which always aroused suspicions. Even then an estimated crowd of 200 followed him uptown towards the police station just in case. He complained bitterly about his treatment even though he confessed that his trip to town was made only to see what all the excitement was about. He found out!

Fisher took the next train back to Crestline.

Another group of nearly 200 went searching for Dowie elders at the homes of Zion members but found none. First they went south-east towards Little Washington and searched the Snyder home and then on to Ballietts. They returned to the city around 7:00 o'clock. It must have been good exercise. No Dowies were found.

Sunday evening several boys were playing around the court house, and began yelling. It had the effect of a riot alarm, and a reporter wrote that within less than three minutes a crowd of 500 rushed to the place. The kids got a good laugh out of it. A bunch of adults that seemed to appear from nowhere took it good naturedly. Well, there really wasn't much to do on a Sunday evening in Mansfield was there?

Such was the situation in Mansfield. Out-of-control mobs were rioting. Church Elders and others were being tarred, feathered, beaten or painted and run out of town. The Sheriff and police were overwhelmed. Taxpayers were nervous about possible law suits. Mayor Brown was under fire from the press, from Dowie and Overseer Piper. The Governor was under pressure to send in the Ohio National Guard, some members of which couldn't be trusted. The Sabbath day found the damned farmers and others standing

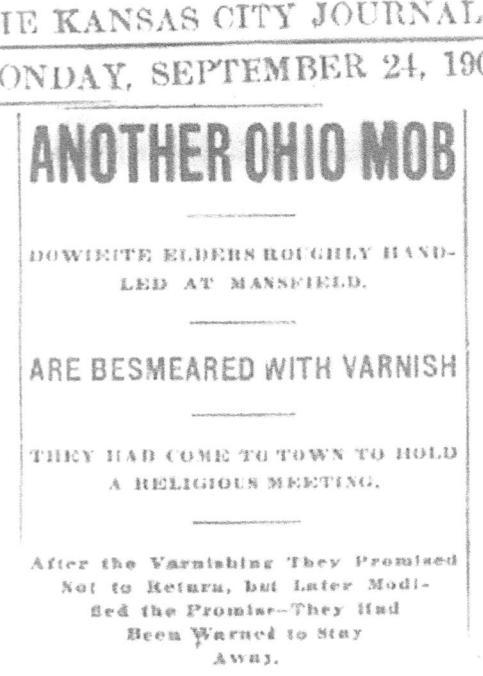
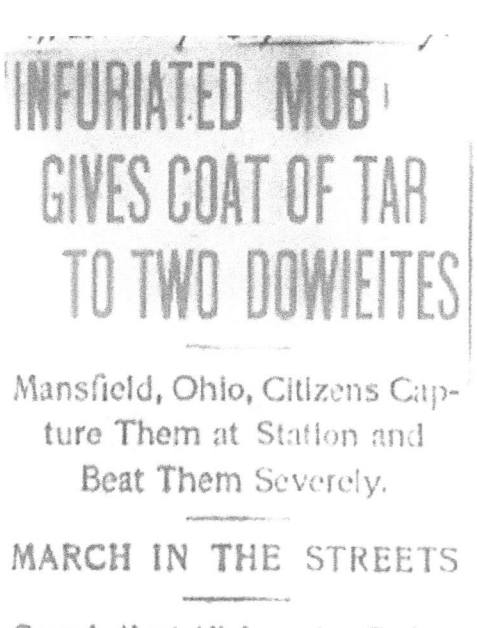

Figs. 83 and 84. Newspapers all across the United States, including these from Kansas City and Philadelphi, reported daily what was goin on in Mansfield. It was a source of considerable embarrassment to city and county officials. (Zion Scrapbooks, Newberry Library, Chicago)

around town grinning just waiting for an excuse to riot. Newspapers from all over the United States were reporting all that was going on which gave Mansfield, and its elected officials a black eye. Local ministers were trying in vain to control their congregations. Two houses had been wrecked by mobs and others were subjected to forced search. Every weekend another train load of trouble arrived at the depot. Lawyers were arguing on the streets. Editorials pleading for law and order were ignored. Bundles of *Leaves of Healing* arrived weekly and healed nothing! Zion Attorney A. A. Douglas carried at least one revolver, sometimes two, because of threats received and stated publicly there would be funerals if anybody started something.

It was one hell of a mess and all because of one man, Chicago's John Alexander Dowie and his Christian Catholic Church in Zion. And at the height of all the turmoil he boarded a ship and went sailing away from it all.

Chapter 8
Dowie Lands in England

When the steamship sailed away from the dock in New York with the Dowie bunch on board there were many with hopes he would never return. His arrival in London was not heralded as a memorable news event by the British even though his Zion movement had reached that country. Only a minimal report was relayed to the United States.

> *Chicago Inter Ocean*, Sept. 1, 1900.
>
> **London, England. John Alexander Dowie of Chicago, who came to England to promote the Zion movement, has been kept busy this week. Although he has not begun real work in London, Dowie is besieged with letters, telegrams, and callers urged him to initiate the Zion movement forthwith. Dowie, however, is going to Scotland for a month's holiday before beginning his campaign. His agents are at work trying to secure a building for the autumn operations.**

Dowie was not a citizen of the United States and was reportedly in a position with the law in Australia that would prevent him from returning to the United States. That could have been more hopeful thinking than fact. He would later return to Chicago.

Dowie was born in Edinburg, Scotland in 1847. By the age of six he had completely read the bible. In 1860 his family moved to Australia but he returned to Scotland in 1867 and entered and studied at the theological seminary at Edinburg and continued his studies in Sydney, South Wales. It was in seminary where he was studying the principals of Congregationalism, that he first found the faith healing theory. While reading his bible he made up his mind that Christ meant to cure the mind as well as the body through prayer and the laying on of hands. He kept his feeling to himself at first as he became a Congregational minister, but let that denominational connection go when he moved back to Australia. While in Sydney he had his first taste of jail for leading two temperance protests without permission from the mayor. He was locked up twice, the second time for 30 days.

His mission in England was to buy a lace factory and move the machinery and a few skilled operators to his new Zion city. This he was able to accomplish, but not without some controversy. The British Government was not happy about the thought of losing an industry to the Americans, but finally gave permission. The US Federal authorities also reluctantly agreed to let the equipment in. Rumors circulated that whole families or most of the population of the town of Beeston southeast of Nottingham were leaving too. The American consul in Nottingham stated that the lace workers would not be admitted to the US. As it turned out less than half a dozen of the highly skilled lace curtain workers went with the machines to set up and teach workers at Zion City. A foreman was promised $50 a week and four twist hands at $35 a week. It was to be the first large scale lace manufacturing industry in the United States.

Chicago Daily News, Oct. 4, 1900

English newspapers continue to attack "Dr." John Dowie and his motives for coming among them, quoting largely from American newspapers concerning his Chicago operations. The efforts of the "general overseer" of Zion have been largely devoted to the area of Beeston, Nottinghamshire, where the Stevenson lace works are, which he recently secured through the marriage of his sister-in-law to the owner of the property and his exaltation to the degree of "deacon" in Dowie's church.

The establishment which is to be removed to Zion City and made the center of a deal involving $400,000 consists of a few machines occupying a corner of the John Pollard factory in Beeston.

DOWIE MOBBED

Dowie began his crusade in England at St. Martin's Hall in London. As was his style, he strongly condemned the doctors and medical profession along with the druggist. All did not go well as he received a rather hostile reception. Perhaps he should have just come to Mansfield:

London, October 19, 1900

The meeting held by John A. Dowie, the Zionist from Chicago, was raided by thousands of Medical students. Groups of them formed in all parts of the hall, bellowed interruptions and jeered in chorus. Mr. Dowie denounced the disturbers and sent for police. The latter enter the hall during a scene of uproar and arrested six students.

Further disturbances took place in the evening. A body of students tried to rush the platform. They threw chairs at Dowie who called upon police and fled by a side door. Police fought their way in and endeavored to expel the rioters, arresting a number. Fighting was then resumed, sticks and chairs being used as weapons. The students tried to rescue those under arrest. Ultimately more police were summoned and the hall was cleared.

Fig. 85. John Alexander Dowie in 1900. (Zion Historical Society)

The London press, which Dowie blasted at the meeting, reported that the audience consisted of "300 old women and 400 medical students from different hospitals." Dowie denounced The Church of England, the Archbishop of Canterbury, the Pope and the Masonic fraternity. He had tried to shut down the protestors but as the paper put it, "He might have well tried to check a cyclone." Dowie lost his temper as usual and implored someone to summon police. Seven "bobbies" fought their way in and dragged three students out. To the voices of students were added the noise of trumpets, whistles and rattles. When the students charged the stage they were met by 50 hired Zion body guards and the fight was on. More arrests were made.

A few days later the protesters returned to disrupt another meeting. While Dowie was attempting to speak, several jokesters stood up at different places in the hall and loudly delivered their own faith healing theories. That attracted clusters around them leaving Dowie's voice almost inaudible. He abruptly left and returned to his £50 a week apartment at the Hotel Cecil.

At the next lecture Dowie arrived in a brougham pulled by two smart horses amid boos from good sized crowd outside. He was escorted up the front steps of the hall by his young male secretary and a well dressed lady sympathizer while 200 policemen stood by in and around the hall to maintain order. No one was admitted to the hall without a ticket which cut out the hecklers. A newsman asked who was paying for all the police?

Fig. 86. The London Star carried this illustration of what they called the "Chicago Mystery Man." His gestures while preaching were master showmanship. (Zion scrapbook, Newberry Library, Chicago)

The Weekly News, Mansfield, October 25, 1900 The *London Daily Mail* devotes an editorial to the denunciation of the authorities for "encouraging and protecting" Mr. Dowie. "If the students had succeeded in ducking this aged fraud" it says, "no great harm would have been done. He is able to rely on the whole strength of the police for no other purpose than to fleece the public. His meetings should be stopped."

The British Weekly devoted six articles as an exposé of the practices of the leader of the Christian Catholic Church. Other publications did likewise and some of their research came from American newspapers. That was how Mansfield notoriety went across the pond.

The London Star, October 24, 1900

When The Star said the other day that in his own country Dowie, the Faith healer, would be tarred and feathered, we were more accurate than we knew. Dowies newspaper reports that at Mansfield, Ohio, the missionaries of Zion have been tarred and feathered. It is a distinction that has been conferred on more honest men. In Mansfield, there are buttons worn with two tar brushes shown in the picture....

Meanwhile Dr. Dowie is traveling in saloon carriages and paying £50 a week at the Hotel Russell. He is a great authority on Biblical examples. Fancy St. Paul staying at the Hotel Russell!

Fig. 87. Dowie needed to be sheilded by police protection when he arrived at a hall in London. His audience was limited by tickets in an attempt to keep out medical students and other hecklers. (Zion scrapbook, Newberry Library, Chicago)

Before an audience in a small town Dowie made another unfortunate statement which found its way back to American papers;

> **I have been accused of being an American freak. I am not an American at all. I am a Scotchman. I am a subject of the British Crown, and proud of it. I object to the constitution of the United States because God is not in it. I prefer the British constitution because it recognizes God. If the United States should declare war against Great Britain, I would go over to Canada and pray for the United States to get licked.**

Dowie baptized 50 men and women in a private bath before he left London. From there went to Edinburgh, Scotland and Belfast, Ireland with plans to visit other cities. Where ever he went, the press and medical fraternity were after him. In a sermon he had this to say:

> **Some people tell me they fast in order to live pure lives. Ugh! If you can only live pure lives by fasting, I pity you. You say you are happy but you are regular scarecrows. I do not take any stock in the Christianity which looks lank and lean and scrappy and hawk like. I'm sure the idea of living inside some of you stinking, drinking, pig eating people is horrible. You smell bad enough outside, but Lord what you are like on the inside. I am getting off a little revenge now about being shut up one night coming from**

Belfast to Liverpool with a whole lot of people of that kind. My, I smelt for a week. Do you think God lives in that! He does not. I had one night of it and that's all I want. God wants to live in a clean temple and He will have a clean temple.

His time in the British Isles did not go well. He cut his trip short and returned home.

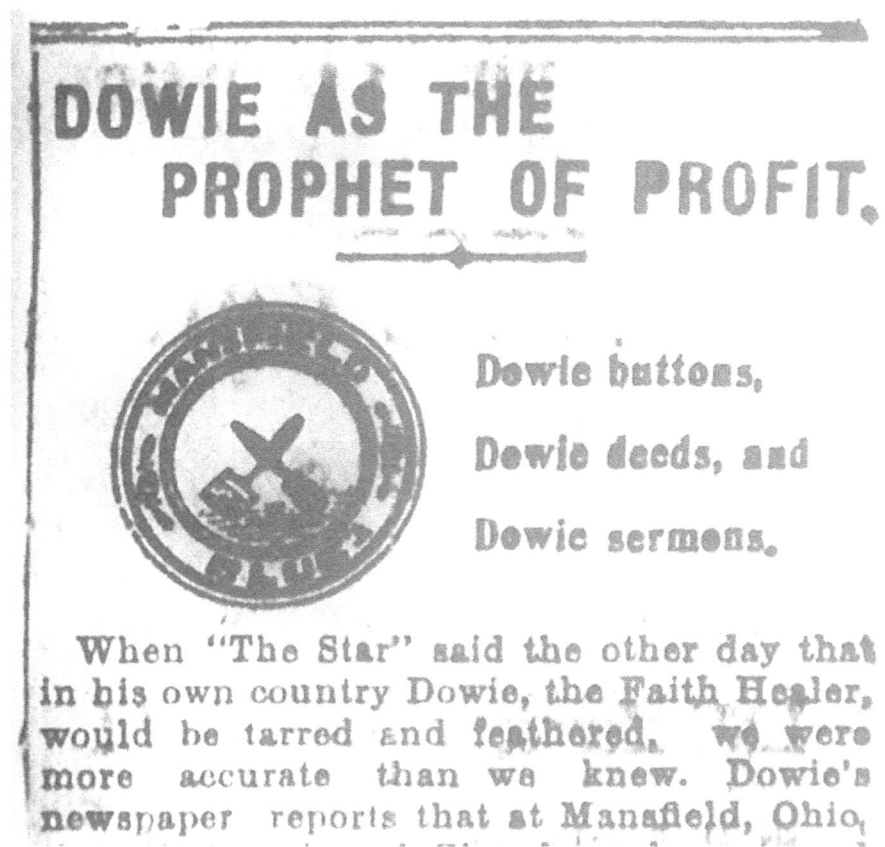

Fig. 88. "Some people tell me they fast in order to live pure lives. Ugh! If you can only live pure lives by fasting, I pity you. You say you are happy but you are regular scarecrows. I do not take any stock in the Christianity which looks lank and lean and scrappy and hawk like. I'm sure the idea of living inside some of you stinking, drinking, pig eating people is horrible. You smell bad enough outside, but Lord what you are like on the inside. I am getting off a little revenge now about being shut up one night coming from Belfast to Liverpool with a whole lot of people of that kind. My, I smelt for a week. Do you think God lives in that! He does not. I had one night of it and that's all I want. God wants to live in a clean temple and He will have a clean temple."

Chapter 9

Mansfield Troubles Continue

Chicago News, **Sept 25, 1900**

Mansfield, O. has varied its usual diversion of painting Dowie elders by giving a couple of them a coat of varnish. Without the excitement of Dowieism Mansfield would be a dull town to live in.

There was plenty more "smokestack" varnish, tar and paint floating around just waiting for the right moment, the right person. For a week things were fairly quiet so newspapers picked up opinions or anything else to keep readers interested.

***Mansfield News*, September 25, 1900**
Al Moore, Lexington correspondent;
There was quite a sensation created here Sunday by the strange and excited actions of an individual who, it is said, was a Dowie elder who had found the climate about Mansfield too torrid for him. He had a grip and trudged wearily into town from the Mansfield road and collapsed quite exhausted on the platform at the depot about 4 o'clock. He had a clerical cast of features and his garb was of quite fine fabric and was in all details of the fashion of a typical Dowie elder. He shook convulsively and cast fugitive glances and acted like a hunted criminal. He asked the road to Galion and when a train left there for the west and spoke in trembling accents. Finally he walked up Main Street and entered Fisher's restaurant and called for a sandwich and he was so nervous that he could hardly eat and his agitation attracted the attention of everybody. He acted like one who thought some avenger was close on his trail and at any moment might wield a knife on him with deadly effect. Finally he rose slowly from his chair and tremblingly grasped his grip and started out with laggard step pursued his way toward Galion.

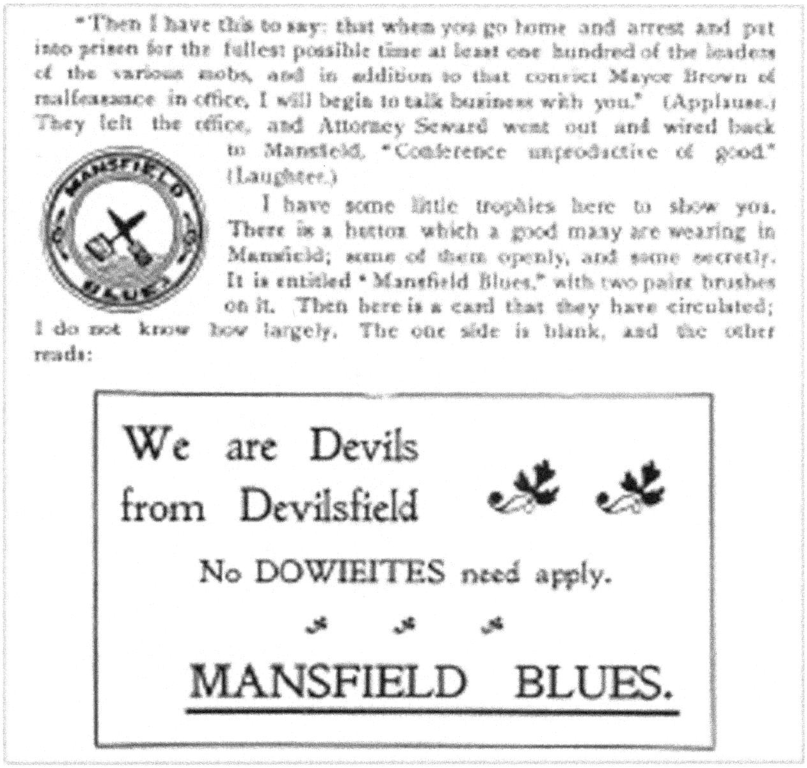
"Then I have this to say: that when you go home and arrest and put into prison for the fullest possible time at least one hundred of the leaders of the various mobs, and in addition to that convict Mayor Brown of malfeasance in office, I will begin to talk business with you." (Applause.) They left the office, and Attorney Seward went out and wired back to Mansfield, "Conference unproductive of good." (Laughter.)

I have some little trophies here to show you. There is a button which a good many are wearing in Mansfield; some of them openly, and some secretly. It is entitled "Mansfield Blues," with two paint brushes on it. Then here is a card that they have circulated; I do not know how largely. The one side is blank, and the other reads:

We are Devils
from Devilsfield

No DOWIEITES need apply.

MANSFIELD BLUES.

Fig. 89. On Sunday, September 30 Overseer Piper addressed the congregation at Zion tabernacle and gave this account of what he said to the Mansfield delegation. His detailed speech was reprinted in Leaves of Healing. (Zion Historical Society)

Something had to be done. A group of Mansfield business and industrial leaders accompanied by lawyers Douglass and Seward went to Chicago to broker a peace agreement with Overseer Piper. The mayor's brother, J. E. Brown, president of Altman Taylor Company, Mansfield's largest industry, Col. B. F. Crawford, president of the National Biscuit Company, and Henry Hedges the local Republican big wig and Chairman of the National Republican Speaker's Bureau, conferred with Piper, but to no avail. At the same time a Chicago paper carried details of the delegation and also a report of the "Mansfield Blues."

The following week Piper tried to pull a fast one. Two Elders by the names Moody and Loblaw arrived by train and were greeted by the usual crowd and police. They were placed in the depot waiting room while awaiting deportation on the next train west when someone noticed another Dowie elder getting off another car. It was Elder Moody who had been in Mansfield before. He was forced back into the rail car and was seen conferring with yet another Elder. All four were sent out of the city which pleased everyone. A policeman went along as far as Crestline.

In the meantime two more Dowie Deacons disguised as farmers, with slouch hats and old clothes, were driven into town from Shelby by two women in a two-seat buggy. S. P. Fogwell and John Rickter attracted little notice and registered at the Vonhof Hotel at 3:30. The clerk didn't know their mission and gave them room 32. Suspicions arose when the women were seen leaving town. Somehow the Deacons were discovered and by 7:00 a crowd equipped with tar, paint and walnut juice gathered outside the hotel covering both sides of North Main. The police arrived and located the Deacons but were unable to persuade them to leave town. That's the way things stood with police and Sheriff Pulver and deputies outside clearing the streets until Landlord Shonfield returned from a trip to

Fig. 90. William Hamner Piper was Dowie's number two man. He was in charge while his boss was away in Europe. An able leader, Piper was often handicapped by Dowie's orders and antics in Leaves of Healing. (Zion scrapbook, Newberry Library, Chicago)

Fig. 91. The author was unable to find an original "Blues" button in any museum or collection in the Richland County area. A single rare example might be worth thousands. (More or less.) This version of the Mansfield logo was clipped out of a Chicago newspaper. (Zion scrapbook, Newberry Library, Chicago)

Zanesville and went to their room, woke them up and ordered them out of his hotel. He didn't want the place to get a bad name.

They refused to go so he called police and they were arrested near midnight and taken to the railroad station and sent west.

It was learned the next day that all six had not exactly received the welcome mat at Crestline (Mansfield always seemed to send its problems over there) and the two had arrived without train tickets. They were arrested and jailed but released the next morning after explaining how they were forced onto the train. The Dowies had been using the Continental Hotel as their headquarters for a couple of weeks and taking Sunday trains to Mansfield. Surprisingly, there were no protests in Crestline and the Crestline Advocate simply reprinted Mansfield news stories.

OVERSEER PIPER MAKES THREATS

Back in Chicago Overseer Piper was leading a service in the Zion tabernacle along with "Dr." Speicher when a telegram arrived from the four Elders kicked out of Mansfield. It hit the church service like a bomb. The *Chicago Inter Ocean* carried this story which was reprinted in the *Mansfield News*, October 1, 1900;

Fig. 92. The Continental Hotel in Crestline also served as a station for two railroads that crossed there. It was noisy but the Dowies got used to it as often as they stayed there. (Crestline Public Library)

Overseer Piper started the attack and the congregation joined in. The meeting was by far the most tempestuous of any of the gatherings that have been held in Zion's tabernacle on Michigan Avenue. The cause of the Dowie's wrath was a telegram from Mansfield, Ohio, received dramatically enough while services were in progress. It was to the effect that the elders who were sent to Mansfield, Saturday had been arrested and deported. The arrest of the four elders balked Pipers plan to get his disciples into Mansfield. Moody and Loblaw were British subjects. It was arranged that two were to arrive on one train and Moody and Loblaw on another. It was the plan, that while police were busy with the first two they would miss the others. Mansfield however had all its police force on duty and nabbed all four. It was this which angered Piper.

Reads from the Bible

Dr. Speicler opened the afternoon services at Zion at 3:00. He began by reading the Bible, a paraphrased part of the text into the following; "And the Lord shall lead his disciples into Mansfield." At the mention of the town the Dowieites began uttering groans and Speicler then ceased reading and launched into the Ohio affair.

"This mob is being urged on by the Masons," he said, "Yes, our enemies are the Masons," shouted the congregation. "They are plotting our destruction,' he continued. "Will they succeed?" "No" answered Zion and Speicler smiled triumphantly.

Then Overseer Piper addressed the congregation. He is a young man and a vigorous talker. In a short time he succeeded in working the congregation into frenzy. "I want to say a few things about Mansfield," he began with a smile. "We have the mayor of Mansfield and the people right where we want them. They are coming to Zion now and asking us to be lenient with that mob. They are asking us to have mercy on a lawless band of men who, headed by two saloon keepers, heaped indignities upon our glorious elders. Last week Attorney Douglas and a committee from Mansfield came to Zion and asked Dr. Speicler and myself to please keep our elders out of Mansfield for three months. At that time they would guarantee us full protection of the law. They wanted us to stay out of Mansfield for three long months!"

"Yes until after the election" interrupted one of the Dowieites. "That's the point exactly," said Piper. "They wanted us to stay away until after the election. Will Zion stay away from Mansfield?" "Never," shouted the congregation. "No, Zion will never stay away from there,' said Piper. "We will keep sending our disciples to Mansfield, even if we all die."

At that point another telegram was handed to Piper which he read and then smiled. It was from Moody and Loblaw explaining they had been arrested and run out of town. Piper explained his plan. Moody and Loblaw were both British subjects and he would appeal to the British authorities for their protection if the Ohio officials wouldn't or couldn't! The British would always protect their subjects where ever they were. That would really embarrass Mansfield and win the fight.

WHY THE ELDERS STUCK IT OUT

When you became an Elder in the Christian Catholic Church you signed all your property and possessions over to the church (to Dowie) and the church provided for the needs of you and your family. Should you disobey church rules or orders from superiors, or for some reason wished to leave the order, you left with the shirt on your back and not much else. It is very doubtful that any of the Elders ordered to Mansfield ever wanted to make a first trip, let alone a second one. In reality, they had little choice. Most had a family to support. They couldn't quit. Dowie ruled with an iron hand.

The first two Sundays in October saw more of Piper's Elders or Deacons arrive and promptly depart with police assistance. The second bunch tried to sneak in, however, with a vaudeville company named "Little Irene." Irene made it but they didn't. They got past police at the station but were spotted at a hotel and escorted to "Pulver's Parlor" and then to the railroad station to be sent west.

Fig. 93. Dr. John Speicher was a Zion General Overseer and a long-time trusted associate of Dowie. He was widely respected in the church. (Century Magazine, Dec 1906)

By Monday, October 15, a cat-and-mouse situation was beginning to develop with several Dowie preachers quietly coming into town. Deacon A.F. Lee was one who did not escape notice and wrote of his experience in *Leaves of Healing*:

> It was somewhere between three and four o'clock when I called at the home of Mrs. Bauer, 194 East Third Street.
>
> I found her confined to her bed by illness, with her open Bible in hand. She and her sister, who was also present, expressed themselves as glad to see me when I made myself known.
>
> I proceeded to read her some encouraging passages of Scripture, but had not gone far when an officer was ushered in by the mother, who, I am told, owns the house and lives with them, but is bitterly opposed to Zion.
>
> The officer laid hold of me in no gentle manner and ordered me to go with him. As I saw that Mrs. Bauer was being much excited, I proceeded to go.
>
> Mrs. Bauer and her sister then pleaded that I pray with them before going, which I asked the officer permission to do. I was refused, and pulled out of the house. The

officer kept his grip upon me and pulled me all the way to the jail as if I had been a criminal.

On reaching the jail he hunted up the Sheriff and left me in his charge, although I was given to understand that I was the city's, and not the county's prisoner. I then telephoned Attorney Douglass, telling him what had happened so that my associates might be informed without making their presence at the Bunswick known.

The Mayor and his attorney came, and in the presence of the Sheriff, several police officers and a reporter for the News. I was asked a few questions as to when and how I came and what my plans were, etc.; also where I had been stopping, to all of which I used discretion in answering.

It was settled that I was to be deported on the Pennsylvania and Fort Wayne 7:50 train to Crestline. I was taken to the depot in a carriage, in company of the Mayor and the Sheriff, who, the Mayor insisted, must go; also two police officers.

Crowds lined the streets and sharp outlook was kept by my escort all the way. When we reached the depot, there was a large and noisy crowd waiting for us; also several more police. I was driven as close to the entrance as possible, taken from the carriage surrounded by police and hustled into the depot to wait for the train, which was a few minutes late.

Fig. 94. The Brunswick Hotel on the corner of East Fourth and Diamond Streets didn't want riot trouble and had Deacon Kessler put out by police. The proprietors didn't want the place to get a bad name. (Phil Stoodt collection)

As I shook his hand I said, "I hope you have repented of your treatment of them," upon which he pretended to be astounded, and then grew sarcastic and insulting in the extreme, and warned me that if I came back I was liable to get my head smashed. In this, one of the police officers joined him.

The Mayor bought and handed me a ticket and in company with Mike Weil—who wore a large Bryan badge—led the police escort which put me on the train. The last named party had the audacity to come on the train, grasp my hand and address me as "old friend" and introduce himself as the "protector" of Elders Basinger and Moot.

As I shook his hand I said, "I hope you have repented of your treatment of them," upon which he pretended to be astounded, and then grew sarcastic and insulting in the extreme, and warned me that if I came back I was liable to get my head smashed. In this, one of the police officers joined him.

In fact, several of these officers have been very insulting to us. One who escorted me to the train yesterday said we called ourselves Christians, but we were worse than the lowest saloon bums.

I was only in Mansfield about one and one-half hours today, Tuesday, October 16th, and was on my way to Mrs. Brent's when I was captured and rushed by several officers down an alley to the Baltimore and Ohio train and sent to Shelby junction, where I took a Big Four train to Crestline.

It became evident that Piper's plan was to flood Mansfield with his Elders and Deacons. Police intercepted a telegram from Piper to Deacon Kessler which read,

Hold services this afternoon between 2 and 3 o'clock at all hazards.

Mansfield Shield & Banner, Oct. 16, 1900 Deacon Kessler returned to the city Monday at noon from Crestline. He was sent out of the city Sunday. Police were notified that he was at the Brunswick Hotel by Landlord Kittle who requested the police to remove him. Accordingly

J. P. Seward, Deputy Sheriff Tom Bell and Officer Wilson went to Kessler's room but he refused them admittance. Threats were made to break down the door but Kessler was obstinate. Finally two employees of the hotel, one a chamber maid, crawled through a window which opened out on a roof shed and unlocked the door and forcibly admitted the callers.

Kessler was taken to a cab waiting outside and driven to the Union depot. When the 10:30 train arrived he was placed on board and the doors held shut by police so he couldn't get out. Kessler was very belligerent. When the conductor attempted to collect Kessler's fare the Dowieite refused to pay and the conductor took his hat for payment. Kessler protested vigorously and said he would complain to the superintendent. "All right," said the conductor, "you can complain to the superintendent but he will give you your hat when you have paid him the forty cents, the amount of your fare."

Deacon Kessler was a newcomer to Dowie's ranks. He was formerly a long-time Methodist minister in Logansport, Indiana, and caused a minor uproar when he left that denomination in January of 1900 and attempted to start a branch of Dowie's church at that town. Several other Methodist clergy persons switched to the Zion movement during that period.

THE SNEAK INS

The next day October 17, Elder E. F. Williams of Chicago rode into town from Crestline on a bicycle. Somebody spotted him and telephoned police. He was refused hotel accommodations and later was captured at the corner of First and Sturges. For a little variety, the police put him on the B&O and sent him to Shelby. He came back the next day walking his bike (somebody flattened a tire) and was escorted out Park Avenue West to the city limits by Officer Huber. It was believed that police did not get hold of more than half of the Dowies trying to find a way into Mansfield. At one Dowie meeting only two men and five women were present.

The following day (Oct. 18) Elder Homer Kessler arrived at the depot and fell into an "infuriated mob" of men and boys. Police located him on North Park Street and started for the railroad station as was the custom. At the station Deputy Sheriff Tom Bell and Dowie attorney A. A. Douglas arrived with a writ fresh from the desk of Judge Campbell. Bell put his hand on Kessler and informed him he was now in the custody of the county. When he tried to hail a cab the mob cursed the cabman and threw stones at his horses. He whipped up the horses and fled. A drunk and the angry mob then followed Bell and Kessler.

Fig. 95. A cartoonist had fun with the plight of Elder Williams in the <u>Mansfield News</u>. (Sherman Room microfilm, M/RCPL)

TROUBLE BEGINS

Mansfield Shield, October 18, 1900

…From that time Deputy Bell was forced to fight his way to the jail followed by the intoxicated ruffian and the crowd. There were cries of "Take him! Kill him! Take him down the track!" It looked as though an effort would be made to take the Dowieite away from the officer. Deputy Bell then deputized a local newsman who had been with Bell at the depot.

Kessler was silent as the deputies hurried him along as best they could. At near west Sixth Street a cowardly ruffian threw a rock with great force and struck Kessler in the back. He only groaned. Deputy Bell protested against such cowardly outrages, but to no avail. Missiles were thrown and Kessler was struck five or six times with great force by rocks and brick bats. The deputies were also were also struck. Deputy Bell received a severe jolt with a stone on the back of his neck which staggered him. When the corner of North Park and Diamond Streets was reached a brick bat hurled with great force struck Kessler in the back and doubled him up with pain. "For God's sake don't kill him," cried Deputy Bell after the brick bat had been thrown. Kessler only moaned. Had the brick struck Kessler in the head it would have crushed his skull like an egg shell. Bell deputized a gentleman in front of the court house and the three, followed by the hooting crowd, hurried Kessler into the jail and breathed a sigh of relief. Kessler was put in the corridor of the jail and locked in for safety while the crowd outside contented itself with yelling.

And then the following telegram was sent:

Crestline, October 18, 1900

W.H. Piper

Reached destination by team five-fifteen this morning. Driven from Calver's by threatening mob. Reentered town. Made several calls unmolested. Learned as was taking train of Kessler's imprisonment.

A. F. Lee

The next morning a hearing was held in Judge Campbell's common pleas court room with the mayor, police, lawyers and a good size crowd present. Judge Campbell announced that an application for a writ of habeas corpus for Kessler would be postponed until the following Tuesday. The police were instructed to send no more Dowies out of the city. That was the word. Kessler was to remain in jail with privileges and Sheriff Pulver furnished him with a cot in the corridor.

Mansfield, October 19, 1900

Dear Overseer Piper: I have visited over one-half of members and held several small meetings. We had meeting yesterday afternoon at Mrs. --'s. We were undisturbed, although two policemen drove past the house and then turned around and drove back to town.

I have not been arrested yet, although I have boldy walked the streets and made my calls.

We cannot stop any more at the Brunswick. It is a trap for us. I was there three days undiscovered.

The mob came out to --'s Wednesday night for me, but I was not there. I went out on Tuesday upon the square, but I was left unmolested. The other men have been again and again arrested and sent out. I know now where most of the people live. They know I am around, but the authorities cannot locate me. I find many fine people here of Zion. I am in the fight to stay and win. God sustains me.   Mark H. Loblaw

Fig. 96. The Richland County Jail, situated next to the courthouse on Diamond Street, was intended to protect the citizens of Mansfield from dangerous criminals, but its use during the summer of 1900, however, was protecting Dowie preachers from the dangerous hands of rampaging citizens. (Robert Carter collection)

A rumor that several Dowie preachers had been seen prompted a crowd of mostly men and boys to search the city but none were found. Apparently it was the old theory if you only saw one Indian there must be 100 more hiding in the forest. To that end the next night what was described as "a rampant mob" of over 200 started searching houses. They had walnut juice and tar ready for use. On Lexington Avenue they forced a search of the John Lape home and from there went south on the Newville road to Frank Daubenspeck's and then next door to the home of John Romer. Romer, who was very ill, protested but allowed a search of his house while he and his wife called police and asked for protection. No one came. Romer said that if anyone came inside his house again it would be over his dead body.

Back to town they again searched the Calver and Leiby houses. They came up dry but it was evidently good physical exercise for all.

Chapter 10
The Turning Point

October 20, 1900, may have been a turning point in the whole Mansfield-Dowie mess. Deputy Sheriff Tom Bell swore out an affidavit against Allen Andrews charging him with obstructing justice by interfering with Bell in conducting his official duty with Kessler.

On that same day Mrs. Lettie Romer with her attorney swore out another affidavit against Elmer Hart and four others whose names she did not know for breach of the peace. Hart was arrested and jailed.

Fig. 97. The October 20, 1900 Leaves of Healing blasted Mayor Huntington Brown for trampling civil rights. It created more hard feelings. (Huntington Brown scrapbook, Sherman Room collection, M/RCPL)

These were the first arrests to be made by a citizen.

> ***Mansfield Shield & Banner***, **October 20, 1900 The ringleaders of the recent outbreaks in Mansfield are now about to find themselves in serious trouble as citizens are beginning to realize they have nothing to hope for from the police protection and are beginning to swear out warrants on their own responsibility. The city last night was in a peaceful condition and there were no outbreaks.**

While in jail Elder Kessler became acquainted with Elmer Hart, the young man arrested for going through George Romer's house searching for Dowie elders. With little else to do Kessler held makeshift church services for his very small but captive congregation, and it was reported that at one time he had Hart on his knees trying to teach him how to pray.

The courtroom was packed on October 23rd when Judge Campbell rendered his decision on the Writ of Habeas Corpus. Kessler was not present and, surprisingly, Mayor Brown sat with the spectators. The Judge denied the writ saying that there was no proof other than the defendant's earlier word that his freedom had been restrained, and the cost of the hearing was to be paid by the defendant. Kessler, under examination, had testified he came to Mansfield just to be arrested and gain an injunction. Neither side was really happy about the outcome. The problem was still there.

Kessler was released and spent most of the next day at the Douglas law office. Then, under the watchful eyes of police, he quietly left town.

THE DEATH OF JOHN SHERMAN

Former US Senator and Secretary of State John Sherman died on October 22. His funeral was to be in Washington with burial in Mansfield on the 25th. He was the Mansfield citizen and statesman most admired. Now he was coming home for the last time. President McKinley and cabinet members, along with many nationally known political dignitaries, would attend the funeral while Mansfield was in an embarrassing turmoil.

Fortunately Elder Kessler was gone. Funeral plans went well and almost overnight volunteers built a huge black-draped memorial arch on the square. The funeral procession would pass through it. Flags were at half staff. By proclamation church and fire bells would toll. Cloth bunting draped the Court House, many businesses and homes. The funeral service was to be held in the Grace Episcopal Church by invitation only.

There were "several thousand" present when the train carrying Sherman's remains rolled into the Pennsylvania, Ft. Wayne & Chicago station. Company M, Eighth Regiment Ohio National Guard, marched to the station without music or drum and deployed along the platform where carriages were standing. Mayor Brown and dignitaries were waiting to receive their deceased and much honored townsman. Survivors of the Civil War Sherman Brigade carried a stand of colors with crepe decorations on their arms. All police were present.

The private car of President McKinley had been attached to the funeral train when it came through Canton. A large delegation of Washington and Cleveland office holders, judges and cabinet appointees were on board, as were members of the Sherman family. Ohio Governor Nash and more elected officials arrived a few minutes later on a Baltimore & Ohio train. After it stopped President McKinley was first to step off escorted by Mayor Brown and a committee of five citizens.

A reporter from the *Mansfield News* described the scene:

> The body of Mr. Sherman was removed from the baggage car. There was absolutely no demonstration of any kind upon the appearance of President McKinley, which was remarked by many. It showed the respect and esteem which the distinguished dead is held by all. A death like silence characterized the whole proceeding with the exception of a few short orders given by the military officers. Everything seemed to move slowly and carefully and this, together with the fact that nearly all business of every kind along the streets to the church was suspended, gave the scene a peculiar feature such as seen only once in a life time.

This must have seemed a radical change from the boisterous crowds and mobs during the previous months. Many would remember it for years.

During the hours the body was lying in state at the church it was

Fig. 98. If Mansfield didn't have enough problems already, the death and funeral of John Sherman put the Mayor and all public officials on edge. A riot during the funeral could be the final blow to Mansfield's reputation. (Sherman Room microfilm, M/RCPL)

10,000 passed by to pay their respects before the funeral.

The next day an unwanted Deacon Kessler showed up during the funeral service, slipped into the church and sat down in a rear pew. His presence drew the attention of people in the crowd outside which was reported to A. J. Baughman, a respected publisher, writer, and co-founder of the Richland County Historical Society. Baughman was in charge of the seating.

The Mansfield Shield & Banner reported the event:

> **Noticing a man sitting at the end of a rear pew who looked like a Dowieite, Mr. Baughman inquired, "Are you a Dowieite?"**
>
> **"I am a deacon of the Christian Catholic Church," replied Kessler.**
>
> **"Then I must request you to leave as none but invited guests are allowed in the church,' said Mr. Baughman.**
>
> **"I'm seated here and I propose to keep my seat. I stand here for my right of American citizenship," replied Kessler.**
>
> **"American citizenship cuts no figure here today and is not the question. You will have to leave."**
>
> **"If I go out you will have to put me out," replied Kessler.**
>
> **Mr. Baughman then held a consultation with the ushers and police but it was not deemed advisable to eject him as it would create a scene.**
>
> **Mr. Baughman then again went to him and said, "If you are a gentleman you would not to try to force yourself in a place where you are not wanted, and you surely would not want to raise a disturbance at the funeral of Mr. Sherman."**
>
> **Kessler picked up his hat and went outside on the step where he stated he would remain. He was then ordered off the steps and went to the curb where he was made to move on by police and was finally was lost sight of in the crowd. Kessler returned to Crestline Thursday evening.**

Fig. 99. Company M, Eighth Regiment of the Ohio National Guard marched quietly to the station for the arrival of Senator Sherman's coffin. It was a solemn occasion with all of Mansfield on its best behavior. (Robert Carter collection)

Mayor Brown had requested all factories and businesses closed during the day of the funeral. Huge crowds respectfully lined the streets to pay their last respects to John Sherman, see his family and catch a glimpse of President McKinley and cabinet members. All went well and there was no disturbance. Mansfield was on good behavior.

A little over a week later McKinley would be re-elected along with running mate Theodore Roosevelt.

On Sunday, October 28, Kessler came back, was nabbed by police, held at the station and deported as usual. Unknown was the fact that another elder from Cleveland by the name of Bouck had been in town since Tuesday and held secret services in homes both in town and the country. He was detected at the Leiby home on Sunday and, as a crowd gathered, police arrived and away he went to the station. Larger crowds were at the station and both elders were put on trains by police, Bouck by force.

Mansfield News, October 29, 1900

"I don't intend to get on that train," said Bouck. Officers Crider and Slaybaugh did not argue the matter with him, but seized him by the arms, dragged him from the waiting room and pulled him through the crowd to the train. He was rushed into the train and others of the police went into the car to see that he didn't get off. Officer Slaybaugh accompanied him out of the city to make sure he didn't return to Mansfield.

When asked if he would come back on the next train he said, 'I will not say when, but I'll come back, I'm not ready to go.' He denounced Mayor Brown and said that he should be impeached.

Things were pretty quiet for the rest of the week but on Sunday November 5, elder Bouck and his wife were spotted with E. H. Leiby in the east end. Leiby took off for parts unknown and the couple were quickly surrounded by an angry crowd and made to understand that the two were leaving town at once. The couple was escorted up Park Avenue East to the

Fig. 100. Services for John Sherman's funeral at the Grace Epicopal Church were attended by invitation only. A huge crowd gathered outside the church and thousands more watched as the funeral procession wound its way through the memorial arch at the Square on its way to Mansfield Cemetery. (Richland County Chapter, Ohio Genealogical Society)

Fig. 101. This photograph was provided by Betty Angle Fox whose father, John Angle, took the picture from his grocery on South Park Street. He exhibited the photograph for years in the front window of his store. The photograph below was provided by Betty Angle Fox whose father, John Angle, took the picture from his grocery on South Park Street. He exhibited the photograph for years in the front window of his store.

Fig. 102. The Mansfield News offered an illustration of how a Dowie elder boards a train. It must have brought a smile to readers. (Sherman Room microfilm, M/RCPL.)

square and down Diamond towards the depot. The woman "engaged in a joint debate with the crowd and used a sharp tongue at a mighty swift rate."

At the depot they were joined by another Dowie elder by the name of Loblaw who was also being forced out.

He had been deported several times earlier. An injunction had been threatened the day before by

attorney Douglas and police were ordered not to interfere. No police officers were in sight. It had been decided by the mayor to let the elders take their chances.

The crowd waited outside the station and when the train arrived the three Dowies made their way through the crowd amid jeers, name calling and threats. The woman boarded the car first. The men made a serious error and turned to argue with the infuriated mob. Bouck, described

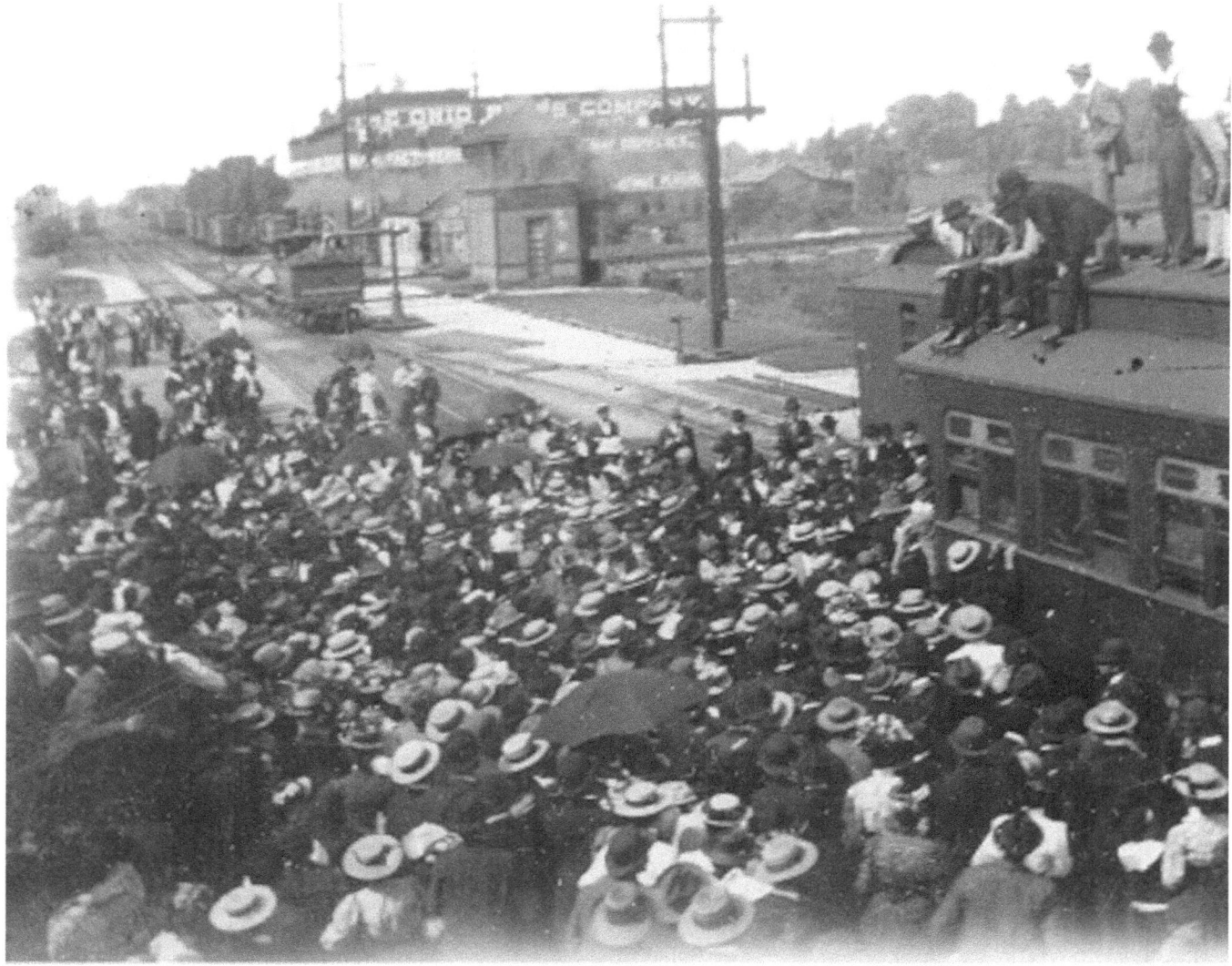

Fig. 103. A crowd similar to this one at the Union Station bid the Dowies, "Don't come back!" and threw rocks to see them off. (Sherman Room collection, M/RCPL)

as a big Scotsman with bushy sideburns, was punched by half a dozen men as he tried to board the car. Loblaw was seized by the clothing, neck and legs while others were punching and kicking him. The two men were barely able to board the train amid cries to "Get him," "Take him off the train," "Paint him," "Get the sucker and fix him." Several men started after them but the train started to move. Limestone rocks were thrown as the train was leaving, and its departure was all that saved the Elders from a paint job.

MEN INDICTED ARRAIGNED

On November 12, 1900 men under indictment by the grand jury were arraigned before Judge Wolfe. Bert Adams, Henry McFarland, William Hartman, Otto S. Miller, Ada Phipps, Samuel Zeigler, and Charles Carroll were indicted and charged with rioting. All were present and pleaded not guilty. Homer Carrothers was also indicted but was out of town. Their appearance bonds were continued.

> "How about the cases of the State of Ohio vs. Dowie, McClurkin, Fisher and Stevens?" inquired Judge Wolfe.
>
> "Your honor, they are out of the state and we have not been able to arrest them," replied Prosecutor Bowers.

It was certain that the others indicted in August including Piper, Fockler, McFarlane and others were out of state except McFarlane of Marion. It was not deemed advisable by the authorities to bring him to Mansfield "owing to the strained condition of affairs in the city."

All this had a profound effect on Mansfield and the riot-prone crowd. On November 26, 1900 Elder F. A. Graves, of Chicago, arrived on Saturday evening and registered at the Vonhof hotel. The next day he conducted church services to a depleted congregation in the Zion tabernacle. It had been returned to them by court order. There was no trouble, no demonstrations.

In January of 1901 the local men indicted were let off easy by sympathetic juries and the judge. The case of William "Red" Hartman was the most serious. As one of the main riot leaders he hired attorney Olin Faber to defend him. Farber pulled a couple of fast ones. First he tried to get the judge disqualified for prejudice. That effort failed. Second, he didn't bring the defendant into the court room or even let him near the court house. Farber then asked each prosecution witnesses to describe Hartman. The descriptions varied and after deliberating over four hours the jury found Hartman not guilty. Older lawyers said they had never witnessed anything like it.

Elmer Hart, another riot leader who led the search of the Romer home, was arrested and faced a possible $300 fine and 30 days in jail. He got off with a warning.

The most serious case involved Allen Andrews. He had been arrested by Deputy Tom Bell and charged with assault, resisting an officer and leading a riot. He presented a pitiful sight in court with his head in his hands and after the judge reviewed local rioting in general gave him a stern fifteen minute lecture. Found guilty, he was given freedom on condition of future good behavior.

With that the Dowie trouble in Mansfield quietly came to an end. Citizens no longer cared to risk arrest and the legal expense of a court trial.

The Zion congregation had been shattered.

The turmoil in Mansfield ended with the arrival of winter. Few wanted to stand outside on the streets or at railroad station looking for the hated Dowies.

It was time for all to go home.

and lawlessness may be established in connection with the recent disturbances.

A FINAL WORD TO ALL CITIZENS.

NOBODY CAN PREDICT WHAT THE NEXT TWENTY-FOUR HOURS MAY BRING TO PASS. IN TIMES OF EXCITEMENT AND UPROAR SUCH AS MAY RESULT IN MANSFIELD, IT IS A DUTY INCUMBENT UPON EVERY CITIZEN TO ACT STRICTLY WITHIN THE LAW, TO BE PEACEABLE AND LAW-ABIDING AND TO REFRAIN FROM ACT OR WORD TENDING TO PROMOTE BREACH OF THE PEACE. THEIR OWN HOMES WILL BE A GOOD PLACE FOR ALL CITIZENS TOMORROW. KEEP AWAY FROM ANY AND ALL PLACES WHERE THERE IS LIKELY TO BE A GREAT CROWD OR ANY SCENE OF DISTURBANCE. PERSONAL CURIOSITY DOES NOT JUSTIFY ANY ONE IN HELPING TO SWELL A CROWD AT ANY PLACE OF PROBABLE DISTURBANCE OR RIOT.

The Hon. E. G. Johnson of Elyria is

Ex-Senator Clark of Montana who

Fig. 104. Final Word to All Citizens

Post Script:
The Rise and Fall of Dowie

Things did not go as John Alexander Dowie planned during his visit to Great Britian. The newspapers and medical community gave him a bad time. He left and moved on to France and Switzerland planting the Zion movement wherever he went. His visit to the Holy Lands and riding into Jerusalem on an ass were postponed. He had kept in touch with the situation back home, particularly Mansfield, and the demands of building Zion City required his personal attention. He returned to Chicago on January 17th of 1901.

Dowie, in addition to his ability to induce people to follow his Zion movement, was a master showman. His carefully orchestrated return to Chicago was reported in the *Chicago Chronicle* January 21st, 1901:

> **The service that followed consisted of "Dr." Dowie in various features. He did the praying, read a scripture lesson, made the announcements and delivered the sermon. He clung to the old methods familiar to Chicago. Occasionally his eyes would roam over the great concourse of people but when he spoke, it was to the newspaper reporters. Whatever he referred to ended with a denunciation of "the generation of vipers," as he terms the newspapers. He prayed for the dying queen of England. He prayed for "all those in authority in this land."**
>
> **After the prayer he denied a report that he had cursed the flag of his native land—Great Britain. He said he still loved his native land, but he had decided to become an American citizen. He announced he proposed to stand trial for the indictment by the Mansfield, Ohio, jury for criminal libel, not only himself, but elder Fockler and Overseer Piper would stand trial in the town which persistently ran out the preachers of Zion. Without apparent appreciation of the humor, he said that Fockler and Piper would go first.**

One person present by special invitation was attorney A. A. Douglass, the Zion lawyer from Mansfield. He later commented that Mayor Brown was prayed for like he had never been prayed for before.

The church services were described as long wearisome affairs which could last four hours or more. One of the "First Apostle's" prayers timed with a watch lasted 45 minutes. Announcements were long and detailed. Scripture reading was as could be expected but Dowie's sermons were most often long, rambling and filled with condemnation of people and institutions who were not in accord with his notions.

ZION CITY IS BORN

Plans for Dowie's dream, Zion City, had started during his absence. Nearly 6,500 acres had been purchased or was being negotiated for at a cost of over a million dollars. This was equal to 10 square miles which bordered on Lake Michigan near the Wisconsin border. The new city was to be laid out by a civil engineer similar to the British flag with avenues running north and south and a grand tabernacle in the center with main avenues running diagonally from there. The Chicago and North Western Railroad ran through the new city.

Early arrivals found living conditions sparse until houses could be built, some living in tents or makeshift shelters. The homes were being built as quickly as possible but construction was hampered by a labor shortage.

Fig. 105. John Alexander Dowie reportedly made this sketch of the temple he proposed to build in his Zion City. A ditch was dug for the foundation but nothing else was ever completed. The site is now a 200 acre golf course. (From the Cleveland Press, Zion scrapbooks, Newberry Library, Chicago)

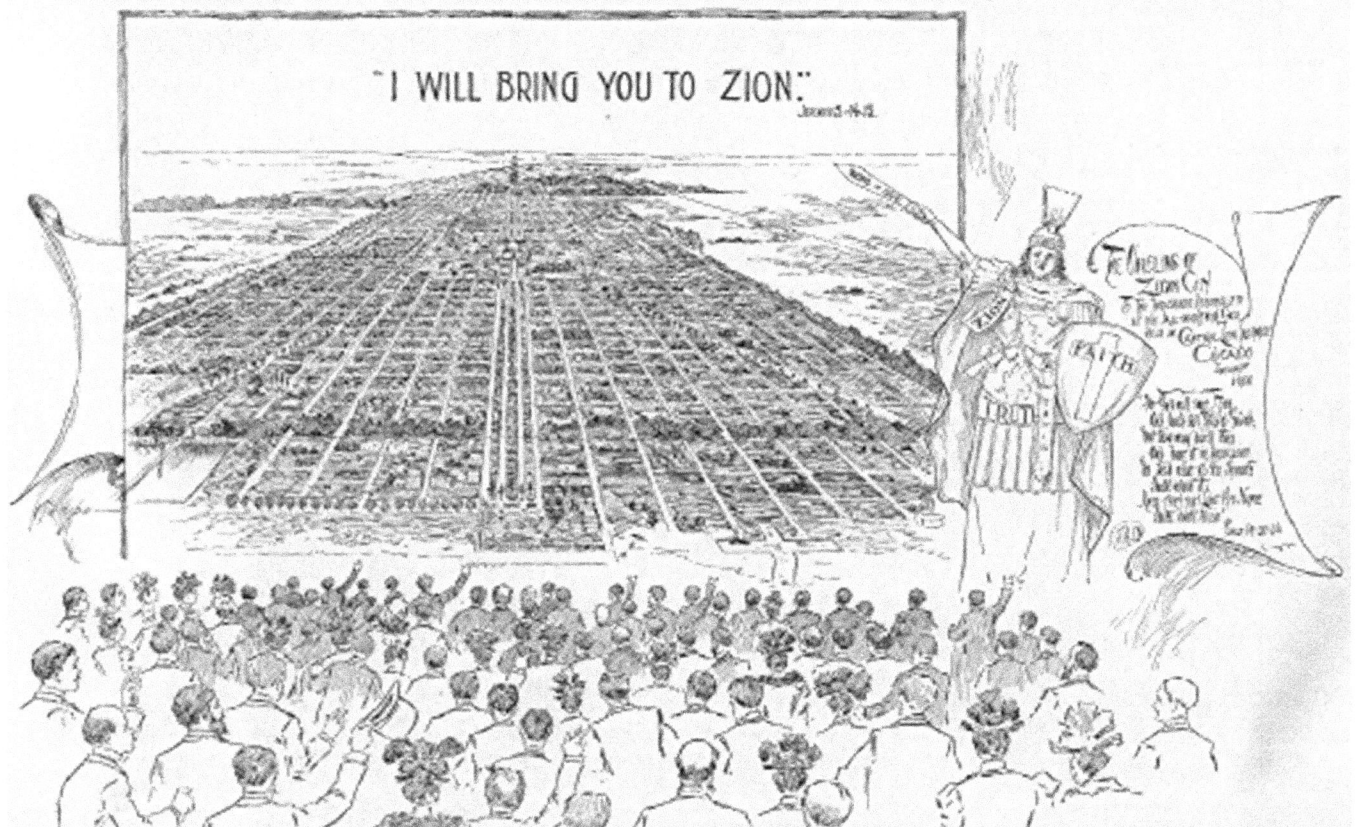

Fig. 106. The grand plan for Zion City was presented to the membership at large in an issue of <u>Leaves of Healing</u>. (Zion Historical Society)

Fig. 107. Zion City is along the shore of Lake Michigan a few miles south of the Wisconsin state line. It was rural farm land when Dowie bought over 6,000 acres. (Zion scrapbooks, Newberry Library, Chicago)

Work on the lace factory building was being rushed but machinery had to be stored in Chicago until it was ready. The English lace workers arrived, some with families, and Dowie had to pay them while they were waiting to start work. That was $3,000 a month. A wide variety of shops, stores, utilities and manufacturing plants were finished or under construction in the fall of 1901. As the city took shape hundreds of Dowie followers bought into their leaders' plan. It was heralded as a God-oriented community with its own Christian schools, college, manual training and Christian art. There was to be no liquor, saloons, drug or tobacco shops, hog-raising or pork use. No dance halls, theaters, doctors' office or hospital was allowed and never would smoking be permitted. Even drinking coffee or chewing gum was frowned upon. Signs at various intersections cautioned that swearing, smoking or bad language was forbidden. Attendance in church was required. At 9 AM daily the power house whistle would blow and all were to stop for prayer until a second blast was given. Photographs reveal there were no fences around the homes. It was a city devoted to God and there was no need to lock the doors.

Dowie owned everything. Houses, factories and stores were all built on lots leased for 101 years from Dowie. "I don't expect to sell a single foot of it," he once remarked. There were lease restrictions that had to be followed. Zion followers were urged to invest in the Zion Bank at 7% interest or buy stock in his new Land Development Company. He always preached to his followers "never borrow money." The huge amount of capital needed for buildings, streets and utilities would have to come from the Zion membership The lace

Fig. 108. Shiloh House was Dowie's grand mansion in Zion City that outdid all others. A three story carriage house for livery and servants was across the street. (Zion Historical Society)

Fig. 109. A 350-room hotel for visitors was built in a little over three months' time. It's construction contributed in part to a labor shortage for home builders. (Chicago Historical Society)

workers produced their first product, a souvenir lace handkerchief, in June of 1901. The machinery was set in a long temporary shed-like building while the main brick building was still under construction. By fall nearly 200 buildings had gone up and hurried construction raced the coming winter. In 1902 hun- dreds more homes sprang up including Dowie's "Shiloh House," a $100,000 25-room three-story brick and stone home designed by a Swiss architect. A

Fig. 110. This first Zion lace sample turned up in Mansfield. Helen Griebling and her late husband Clarence bought it years ago at an antique sale but knew nothing of its history. The lace is shown near actual size.

separate but similarly designed three-story carriage house with horse stalls and apartments for drivers, caretakers and families was next door. The carriage house was grander than most Zion City homes.

A 5,200 seat tabernacle was built, as was a huge four-story 350 room frame hotel for visitors. A large bakery, furniture works and profitable candy factory provided employment for many. There was also an electric plant, lumber mill and the Zion publishing house which had been moved from Chicago. The lumber yard received up to a dozen carloads of lumber daily and a Zion brick kiln supplied builders. It was a growth unlike any other American city.

ELIJAH THE SECOND

On June 2, 1901, in the Chicago Auditorium before 7,000 of his followers, Dowie cobbled together a series of scriptures and justifications in order to claim that he was the "Messenger of the covenant," Elijah II. From the book of Malachi, Dowie stated that Elijah The Restorer was the first with John the Baptist being a second. As Elijah The Restorer he claimed his record of faith healing and success in restoring the church was his "divine commission from God." He believed he would be known as "Elijah II."

This did not set well with everyone, particularly those few with clerical backgrounds. They failed to follow his reasoning and after some research and soul searching, they left Zion as did others. At a rather long four hour conference meeting of 258 attendees the next day chaired by Dowie, only five voted against his "Elijah II" confirmation. All five were promptly expelled from the church by the General Overseer. A few newspaper reporters questioned his mental status.

In the spring of 1902 tragedy struck when Dowie's daughter Esther was badly burned by the explosion of an alcohol burner she was using at the University of Chicago. No medical assistance was allowed for her, only prayers. She died a very painful death after confessing she had sinned: she had tasted liquor. Thousands attended her funeral, many coming to Zion from Chicago by two special trains. A grieving father preached her funeral.

Dowie managed to create huge financial problems for Zion City. He mounted a "New York Crusade" in the fall of 1903 that was conducted in both Madison Square Garden and Carnegie Hall. His mission was to "evangelize" New York City. Ten special trains of ten cars each with sleepers attached to the rear from several rail roads would deliver his faithful to that place. "Elijah II" would arrive first in his private railcar. His gangs of "70" (groups of 70 trained volunteer evangelists) would scour the city, knock on every door, speak on street corners and hand out Zion tracts. They were to recruit thousands of new members and hoped to raise a reported $5,000,000.

The press was not kind to the invasion, called Dowie a fraud and there were trouble makers during services. Groups of students and others walked out while he was speaking. At times 400 police were present to maintain order. Really upset with the press at one service, Dowie ordered guards to "clear the tainted vipers out of here. Be careful how you handle them, not to get any of their filth on you....Now get out, you mean dogs, you yellow scoundrels I will have no more of this. I'm paying for this place, you liars. This is my building. Hurry up guards: The sight of them disgusts me. Don't waste any restoration talk on them. They have sold their souls to the devil. I never hope to convert a reporter. They would be backsliders."

During one meeting he totally lost his temper and resorted to vulgar language.

At another service Dowie made the confession that John Murray Dowie was not his father. His real father was a British Army officer. This sent a shock wave among his followers. During an interview Dowie had also expressed the ambition to convert the Pope in Rome. That too would also raise more than a few eyebrows. Newspaper reporters questioned his motives and mental condition.

Things did not go well in New York. The expense of transporting, feeding and housing nearly 3,000 Zion followers cost over $300,000 at a time Zion was in critical financial straits. The Herald of Arlington Heights, Illinois commented "he didn't take in enough to pay his hotel bill." The crusade failed to meet expectations and was considered a failure. Many of his upset and disappointed supporters went back home before it was over.

Fig. 111. The General Overseer was evidently on a giant ego trip when he donned this elaborate "Elijah II" costume. His actions raised doubts in some minds, but to criticize would lead to expulsion. (Zion Historical Society)

Passes Through the City in Style Like A Potentate

Mansfield News **November 10, 1903**

There have been several rumors recently to the effect that Alexander Dowie would pass through Mansfield, but it was not until Tuesday afternoon that the distinguished Elijah II did go through Mansfield on his way back to Zion near Chicago.

Dr. Jack Dowie passed through Mansfield shortly after dinner Tuesday on the Baltimore and Ohio No. 7. This train is due here at 10:35 a.m. but was two hours late. Dr. Dowie traveled in one of the finest private Pullman cars and had about a dozen persons with him, presumably members of his own family and the high dignitaries in his church. When the train reached this city they were having dinner served to them in the private car. Several of the Dowieites came to the window and stuck their heads out and gazed at what they could see of Mansfield. Jack Dowie disdained to look upon "Devilsfield," but was plainly seen sitting in the car. Nobody knew Dowie was coming through Mansfield and consequently there was nobody at the depot.

Fig. 112. Only the <u>Butler Enterprise</u> and the <u>Mansfield News</u> reported Dowie passing through on the B&O in his private railroad car. One wonders if a crowd would have formed had they known he was coming, or if interest had passed. (Zion Historical Society)

Perhaps that was best. On his way home through Ohio he would have passed quietly through Zanesville, Newark, Mt.Vernon, Mansfield, to Willard, then on west to Chicago.

What Did He Do With All The Money?

Mansfield News, December 3, 1903

It is declared by the receivers appointed by Zion City that the affairs of Dowie are in a worse condition than first thought. It was the opinion that the liabilities of Dowie would not amount to $350,000. It is now admitted by the receivers that the claims against him for merchandise alone will aggregate $500,000 and in addition to this amount there are mortgages on his property in Zion City for $125,000 which are due the first of the year and he owes his brother-in-law $100,000 making a total of $725,000. The receivers found one of Dowie's banks in operation and put an agent in charge and closed the doors.

While Dowie was preparing to leave for Mexico in September of 1905 he suffered a stroke and was partially paralyzed. A second stroke in December left him unable to walk. This raised some doubts in the minds of followers. Dowie always preached illness was the result of sin. Was there sin in Zion? What could their "Elijah" have done?

THE BEGINNING OF THE END

A new General Overseer to look after the affairs of Zion in Dowie's absence was Wilbur Glenn Voliva from Australia. He had been sent there by Dowie in 1901, had done very well in expanding the church, and impressed the First Apostle with his leadership ability. Brought back to America he was now in charge and Dowie gave him Power of Attorney before he left for Mexico in December of 1905. Dowie had found the southern climates more enjoyable than the Illinois winters.

The new thirty-six year old Voliva soon assessed the state of the church and its financial affairs. In one of his first sermons in the Zion Tabernacle he laid out a new order and openly condemned Dowie's conduct and monetary mismanagement. The top leaders who had simply been "yes men" to their absent leader started to fall in line behind Volvia. The membership too began to listen and understood that change was necessary.

Even if he couldn't walk Dowie must have been hopping mad when word of this reached him. From Jamaica, where he was vacationing, he sent a letter demanding the resignation of all officers who did not support him and especially financial manager Alexander Granger. Several of Dowie's checks had come back marked "no funds." It is recorded that at one time his accounts were overdrawn by $400,000.

It was rumored that he had talked of a polygamous colony in Mexico, and a young woman who lived next door to Shiloh House was seen riding with him in his carriage. In that Victorian era such conduct raised eyebrows. Elder Jane Dowie reported she had found the two "together" on a couple occasions and it was later found he had given money to several young women. Ever critical newspapers once more questioned his sanity and moral conduct.

Dowie came back to Chicago storming mad claiming that as leader of the Christian Catholic Church he alone owned Zion and all its assets. Volvia, with Dowie's power of attorney, anticipated that the trouble would wind up in court and sold all of Zion to Alexander Granger for one dollar! Dowie was out!

The bitterly fought question of who really owned Zion landed in court where the judge ruled that the First Apostle was not the owner, only a trustee. The people could decide who would lead Zion. The judge however did grant him the right to live in Shiloh house and that's where Dowie would spend the rest of his days. He had become estranged from his wife and son who, seeing the writing on the wall, joined Volvia fearing they too would be ousted if they didn't. As his health declined he only preached to small groups of his still faithful at Shiloh House on Sundays.

Wilbur Glenn Volvia took over and with 6,000 remaining members renamed it the Christian Catholic Apostolic Church. Bankrupt, it returned to a more simple operation and was run by a cabinet rather than one man rule. The choir robes were gone and Dowie's name was painted over wherever it appeared. Volvia would run it with a steady hand until he

Fig. 113. The high point of Dowie's career was his return to Zion City in 1904. This photograph of the grand reception was taken from an aerial balloon. The story goes that on this day as the balloon was being prepared for launch the prayer whistle blew and everybody let go of the ropes to pray. They nearly lost it. The hotel is shown on the left, administrations buildings on the right. (Library of Congress)

died in 1942. Surprisingly, shortly before he died he confessed he had embezzled large amounts of church funds. It too went broke and dissolved. There had been several splits within Dowie's ranks but Volvia had held the largest segment together.

Mansfield Weekly News, March 14, 1907

John Alexander Dowie, at one time one of the most successful imposters along alleged religious line known in the last century, has made an ending of life, his death coming at Shiloh House, in Zion City, Saturday morning, after failing of physical and mental facilities that has existed for several years.

A few years ago Dowie, who was a man of unquestioned ability, was at the heyday of his powers. His followers were many and zealous, his sway practically absolute and the outpouring of "tithes" remarkable.

Fig. 114. The sprawling lace factory was much larger than was ever needed. The venture into lace manufacturing by Dowie never reached its potential due to poor financial management and chronic cash shortages. The building still stands today, without the tower. (Zion Historical Society)

But Dowie became too ambitious. He claimed too much. Even the credulity of his most zealous supporters was tasked too much by his various claims of reincarnation. Dissensions arose, wife and son deserted him, jealous aspirants for honor and power—and tithes—vied with him for control. Financial troubles came upon Zion and the old man, broken in health and spirits, saw his once staunchest followers forsake him. He has been in late months barely tolerated in Zion, although a few of the original Dowieites stuck to him till the last.

His great achievements of former years, his wonderful power over men constitute a remarkable chapter in the story of the many religious delusions which at various times have influenced mankind.

While Dying He Cursed His Foes

Richland Shield and Banner, March 15, 1907 Chicago.

Six weeks before he died, John Alexander Dowie, founder of Zion City, prepared his own funeral sermon. Thursday he was buried in Mt. Hope cemetery, Zion City, but his last message was not read to his followers. Leaders of the religious community founded by Dowie decided that the sermon would still further estrange the factions into which the believers in Dowieism are divided.

In place of the posthumous sermon, Judge Barnes, a lifelong friend of Dowie, and an overseer of the church, preached a simple sermon in which he extolled the dead man.

Although the sermon prepared by Dowie was not used in the funeral, it was given out for publication. The document makes it plain that Dowie did not forgive his enemies before he died, as he lashes those who ousted him from control as "dogs of hell."

Dowies wife and son were not present when he died nor did they attend his funeral. He had not forgiven them. He was buried in a simple plot in the Zion Lake Mound cemetery. A very plain white round top slab marker about four feet high contains only one word, "Dowie." A few feet away next to a low marker for his daughter Ester, a similar small stone about two feet wide is inscribed with but two words, "John Alexander."

The man who lived so lavishly left with a simple reminder of his existence. A century later both he and the embarrassing riotous behavior he caused in Mansfield are all but forgotten.

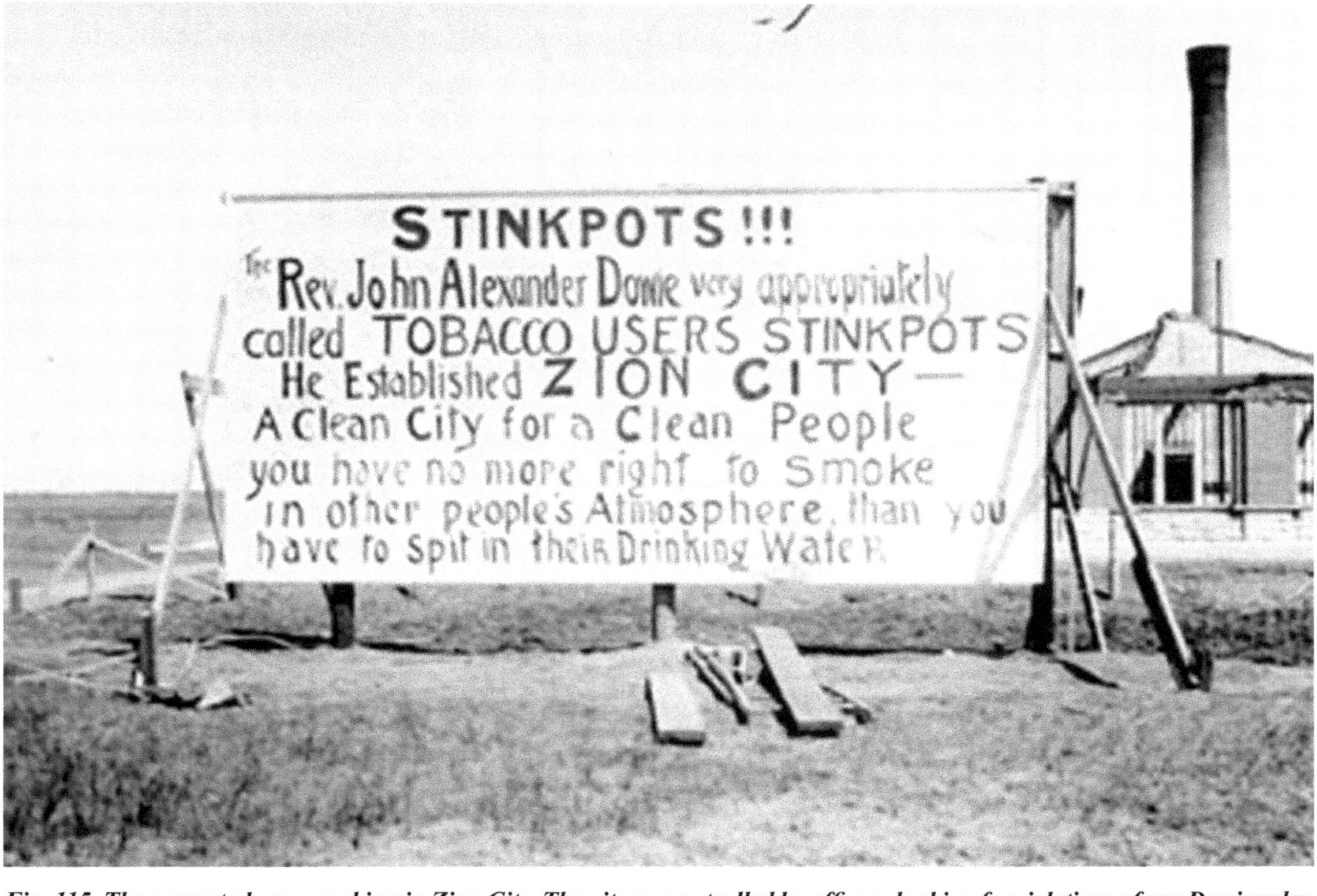

Fig. 115. There was to be no smoking in Zion City. The city was patrolled by officers looking for violations of any Dowie rules. Skipping church, reading out-of-town newspapers or swearing brought big trouble. Signs everywhere reminded of the rules. As late as 1920 a man was stopped by police and arrested for smoking while driving his car. (Chicago Historical Society)

The Last Word:
Glorious Victory

Reverend Cyrus B.Fockler, the one who was to blame for starting all the embarassing riots, wrote the following in the January 12, 1901 edition of *Leaves of Healing:*

Mansfield, Ohio.
Rev. Cyrus B. Fockler, Elder-in-Charge.

Zion's wonderful fight and glorious victory in Mansfield made a deep impression upon the citizens of that place.

With the passing of mob rule, the days of intense excitement and bitter, furious hatred, has come a reaction of calm thought and reflection. Men and women with reason see that Zion cannot be all that her enemies have called her; that in order to fight such a battle and win such a victory, she must have extrodinary qualities.

With this calm thought, there has come a desire to know the truth about Zion.

This was most clearly shown on the occasion of the visit of Deacon John H. Sayrs to Mansfield on Lord's Day, December 30, 1900. Deacon Sayrs took with him a large number of copies of *Leaves of Healing*, Volume VII, Number 9, the edition containing the portraits of the men who had suffered and conquered at Mansfield, and a brief resume of the fight and the victory.

Fig. 116. Dowie men who "suffered and conquered" at Mansfield.

When he offered these at the Erie depot, the scene of so much of the persecution, the place where so many of Zion's ministers suffered violence, the crowd rushed for them and he distributed fifty in a short time.

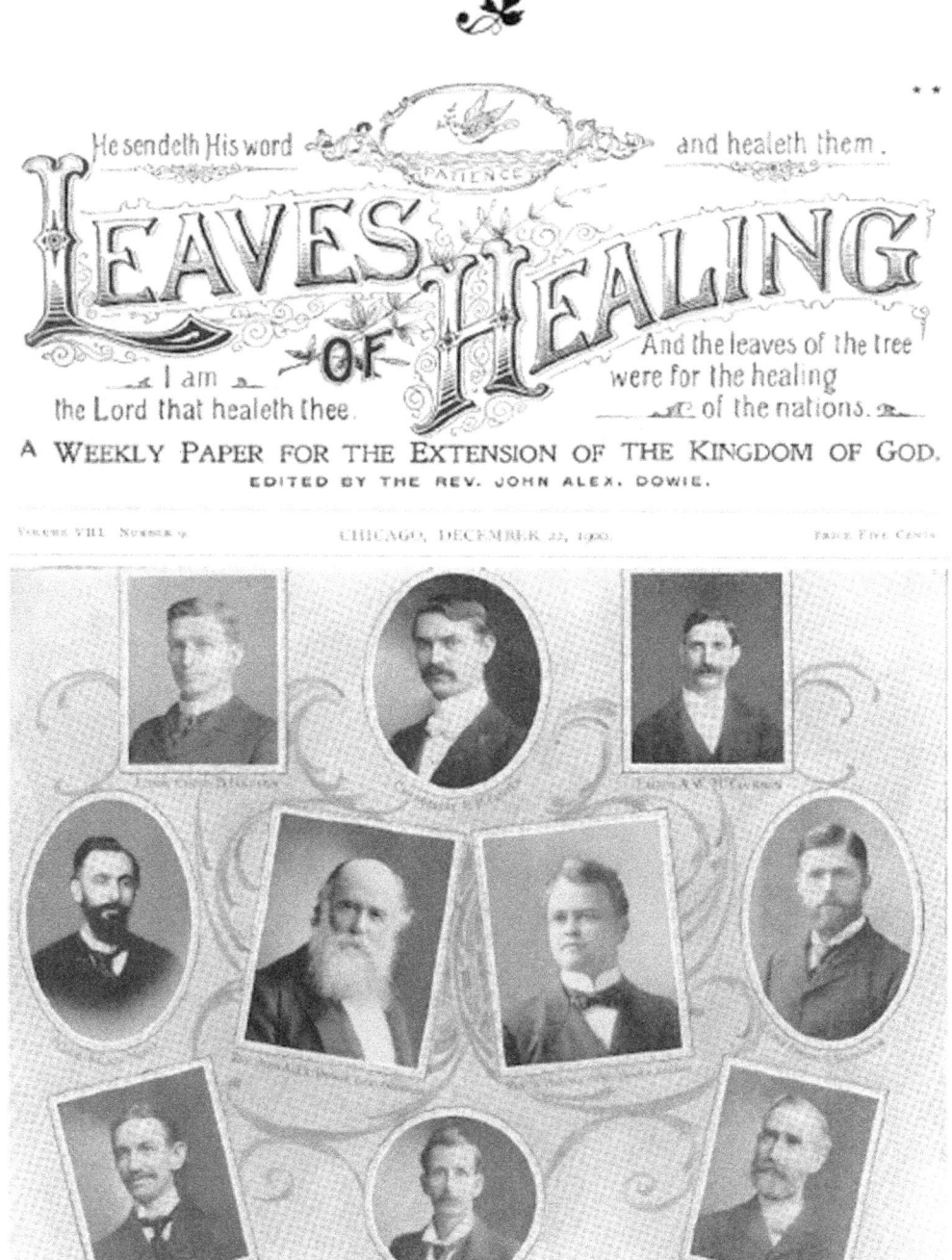

Fig. 117. More Dowie men who "suffered and conquered" at Mansfield.

INDEX

Ashland Times 35
B&O Station 35
Barret, Chief James 61-63
Bassinger, Elder Ephraim 63, 66-70, 73
Bauer, Mr & Mrs Charles 6-8, 15, 87
Baughman, A.J. 96
Baughman, Dr. 10
Bell, Tom 9, 25, 57, 87, 90, 93, 100
Boles, Dr. 1
Bowers, Prosecutor 5-7, 31, 38, 55, 75, 100
Brinkerhoff, Judge 10
Brown, Huntington xi, 2, 7, 8, 10, 51
Brown, Huntington (Scrapbook) 22-23, 44, 47-48, 51, 57, 63
Brunswick Hotel 32, 88-89
Bushnell, Coroner 6, 9, 75
Calver, Frank 60
Cappeller, W.S. 15, 38
Carter, Mary Pulver xiii, 27
Casino, North Lake Park 4, 6
Chicago Chronicle 73, 105
Chicago News 83
Chicago Tribune 15
Christian Catholic Church xi, 3-4, 23, 44-45, 48, 60, 72, 80, 87, 96, 109
Clark, Police Chief 7, 13, 19-20, 25
Columbus Citizen 46, 92
Company M, Ohio National Guard 32, 37-38, 57
Continental Hotel, Crestline 35
Craig, Dr. 1, 6, 15, 75
Dell, "Doss" 14
Dell, Mrs. Frank 7, 9-10
Dinius, Elder W.O. 57-58, 60
Douglass, A.A. 2, 11, 17, 20, 31-32, 38, 58, 60, 66, 71, 84, 102
Dowie, John Alexander xi-xii, 1, 3-5, 6, 8, 10-11, 13, 15-16, 19-23, 26-28, 30-38, 40-55, 57-63, 65-73, 75-81, 83-94, 96, 98-111
Faber, Olin 27, 102
Fisher, Evangelist E.P. 11-12, 19-20, 23-29, 31, 39, 41, 75-76, 83
Fockler, Cyrus 1-2, 4, 6-12, 14-20, 22, 26, 30, 32, 56, 60, 100, 102
Frederick, Lidia 24, 28-29
Frye, George 2
Hartman, "Red" 23, 56-57, 72, 100
Jerusalem 53-54
Kansas City Journal 76
Kerr, W.S. 37
Kessler, Deacon 88-91, 93-94, 96-97
Laver, George 9-10
Lawrence, William 10, 19, 30

Leaves of Healing 9, 11, 19-20, 22-23, 28-29, 34, 51, 57, 62-63, 77, 84, 87, 93, 103, 112-113
Leiby, Enoch, Mr & Mrs. 8, 58, 60, 63, 66, 69-71, 73, 92, 97-98
Mansfield Blues iii, 28, 60, 84
Mansfield City Prison 15-16, 26-28, 61, 74
Mansfield Daily Shield, Shield & Banner 1, 4, 6-8, 10, 24, 28-31, 36, 58, 60-61, 71, 73, 89, 91, 94, 96
Mansfield News 2, 17, 27, 30, 35, 54, 59, 61, 63, 66, 71, 75, 83, 85, 90, 95, 97-98, 107-108
Masonic Order 45, 49, 51, 57, 79
McClurkin, Elder 24-26, 28, 79
McCrory, Robert 34, 47
Mcfarlane, Elder 38, 100
McKinley, President William 32-34, 94-95, 97
Moore, Al 2, 83
Moot, Elder Silas 23, 57-58, 60-61, 73, 75, 89
Nash, Gov. George xi, 20-21, 25, 30, 32, 34, 37-38, 57, 72, 95
News Democrat, Canton 16, 54
Ohio State Journal 38
Pawnee Bill's Wild West 11
Piper, William Hamner 20, 22-23, 28, 31, 35, 37, 39-40, 42, 57, 59-61, 66, 70-72, 75-76, 84-87, 89, 91, 100, 102
Philadelphia North American 75
Pulver, A.B. "Barney" xi-xii, 8-9, 20-22, 25-28, 31-32, 36-39, 42. 56, 60, 63, 75, 84, 87, 91
Roderick Lean Farm Machinery 25
Seward, James 31, 35, 58, 60, 66-71, 75, 84, 89
Sherman, Senator John 9, 94-97
Speicher, Dr. 85, 87
Stevens, Elder 20, 24-27, 31, 100
Strauch, David 58
Sylvester, Bill 75
The Cleveland World 63, 67
The Democrat, Grand Rapids 46
The London Star 8
The Times, Louisville 53
Tremont House 33, 36
Union Station 33-34, 39, 69, 73, 99
Volvia, Wilbur 108-110
Vonhof Hotel 11-12, 20, 32-33, 58-59, 61, 84, 100
W. C. T. U. 38
Weil, Mike 75, 89
Williams, Elder E.F. 90
Wolfe, Judge 37-38, 55, 60, 66, 100
Zion City 45, 50, 78-79, 102-106, 108-111
Zion Tabernacle, Chicago 43, 45-46, 48-50, 66, 71, 85-86, 103
Zion Tabernacle, Mansfield 4, 6-7, 9, 19-20, 278, 37, 73, 100, 105, 108

Also Available from Turas Publishing by Robert A. Carter

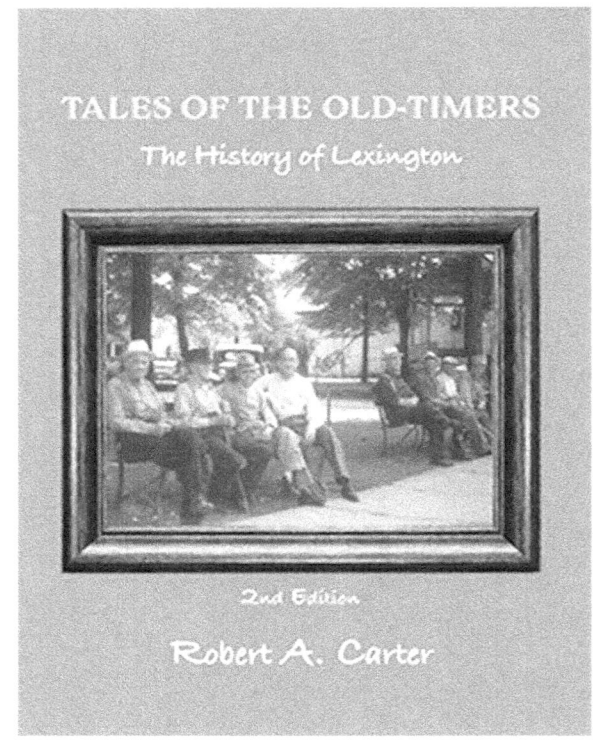

$29.00

https://turaspublishing.com/product/water-powered-mills-of-richland-county/

$26.00

https://turaspublishing.com/product/ tales-of-the-old-timers//

The Author

Robert A. Carter was born in Mansfield, Ohio, in 1935, and graduated from Lexington High School in 1954. Married with 5 children and 10 grandchildren, 3 great grandchildren. He currently lives in Mansfield with his wife Jackie. He is a member of the Richland County Chapter of the Ohio Genealogical Society, the Ohio Historical Society and the Society for Preservation of Old Mills (SPOOM). Since 1964 he has written six local area history books, including *1964 Lexington Sesquicentennial booklet; The Sandusky Mansfield & Newark Railroad* (2002); *Tom Lyons The Indian That Died 13 Times* (2003); *Tales of the Old-Timers – The History of Lexington* (2007); *The Mansfield Riots of 1900* (2009), and *Water-Power Mills of Richland County* (2016).

As of 2024 he continues to write articles for the *Tribune-Courier*.

www.ingramcontent.com/pod-product-compliance
Lightning Source LLC
Chambersburg PA
CBHW042353070526
44585CB00028B/2907